Japan's International Agenda

Japan's International Agenda

Edited by Yoichi Funabashi

A Japan Center for International Exchange Book

NEW YORK UNIVERSITY PRESS
New York and London

New York University Press
New York and London

Library of Congress Cataloging-in-Publication Data
Japan's international agenda / edited by Yoichi Funabashi.
      p.   cm.
   Includes bibliographical references and index.
   ISBN 0-8147-2613-5
   1. Japan—Foreign relations—1989–   2. Japan—Foreign economic
relations.   I. Funabashi, Yoichi, 1944–   .
DS891.2.J38   1994
327.52—dc20   93-40004
                     CIP

New York University Press books are printed on acid-free paper,
and their binding materials are chosen for strength and durability.

Manufactured in the United States of America

c   10   9   8   7   6   5   4   3   2   1

Contents

Foreword

Tadashi Yamamoto

In January 1990, the Japan Center for International Exchange (JCIE) launched a new, independent research project under the title "Japan's International Agenda." Involving younger Japanese scholars, this project was intended to provide an indigenous reassessment of Japan's national interests in the context of a changing international environment and to promote policy debate on its international role within Japan and in its major partners. Research was to cover eight topical areas of security; relations with socialist countries; macroeconomic policy; structural adjustments; trade policy; economic cooperation; science, technology, and environment; and the relationship of domestic politics to foreign policy.

The project was based on two premises. The first premise was that changes in the international environment and Japan's economic success and broad interests require that Japan assume a new international role. In the 1980s, Japan became a truly global economic power, and this happened at a time of increased strains on world systems. The "Japan problem" school, in fact, links these two developments, arguing that Japan's economy and political system are so constructed that Japan cannot be dealt with within the framework of the postwar international institutions. Others see Japan more benignly as "a power without purpose." Clearly Japan must realize that it is both possible and necessary for Japan to play a major leadership role in shaping the international institutions of the future.

The second premise was that the Japanese domestic political processes constitute one of the major constraints on Japan in accepting its new international responsibilities. Japan's political system, in contrast to its economy, has been slow to change, allowing entrenched groups to protect their interests. Recent political developments have brought the Japanese political system to the brink of crisis, encouraged reform-minded activists within the ruling party, and fostered debate about possible new political alignments. These developments have profound implications for Japan's foreign policy that need to be systematically explored. The research, therefore, would also focus heavily on the relationship between domestic political change and a new international agenda. Research in each topical area would address the question of what kind of domestic political change is needed to implement new policies.

Over the past decade, Japan has been examining its international agenda in an exploratory fashion. The effort has been stimulated by external pressures for Japan to assume more financial burdens, and has evolved in a piecemeal and tactical fashion around the question of "managing foreign pressures." To date, the exploration of concrete policy alternatives has been largely carried forward by bureaucrats, those traditionally responsible for public policy in Japan. The lack of a clear set of foreign policy objectives, however, has made it impossible for the bureaucracy to play its previous role as the arbiter of public interests. There is increased recognition that in a more pluralistic society, nongovernmental public policy specialists are needed to provide a more integrated and longer-term vision of foreign policy goals.

In this policy environment, we believed, first, that the Japan's International Agenda project could make a distinctive contribution to domestic public education and foreign policy debate. Second, we believed the project could also help Japan make substantial contributions to international policy debate on the broad questions of strengthening institutions to preserve security and promote trade and development. Third, we hoped the project would enable scholars and experts in North America, Europe, the Asia-Pacific region, and elsewhere to engage in substantive dialogue on critical public policy issues with their Japanese counterparts. I believe I can proudly report to readers of this volume that these three objectives have been successfully achieved; we hope that the publication of this volume and its sister version in Japanese, *Nihon Senryaku Sengen,* will contribute to the international as well as national debates on this topic and that the policy-oriented dialogues with our overseas counter-parts have been promoted through such fora as the Trilateral Commission Tokyo Plenary Meeting in 1991, the Thirteenth European-Japanese Conference in April 1991, and the Eighth U.S.–Japan "Shimoda" Conference of November 1990, all of which used some of the draft papers written for this project as discussion papers.

The contributors to this publication are younger Japanese nongovernmental foreign affairs specialists, each with considerable international experience and committed to the belief that significant policy reforms are needed. As the organizer of the overall project, I sincerely hope that this volume outlines an agenda that a new generation of Japanese political thinkers believes is necessary and feasible as Japan prepares itself for a leadership role in the twenty-first century.

Preface

Yoichi Funabashi

It was in the fall of 1989 that I had a conversation with Tadashi Yamamoto, president of the Japan Center for International Exchange (JCIE), which later resulted in the Japan's International Agenda project, the forerunner of this volume. We were then witnessing the end of the Cold War world system, and the shape of the subsequent world order was totally uncertain. In this situation, we agreed, Japan would have no choice but to comprehensively review its foreign policy. We further agreed on the need to study the new international environment and its effect on the fundamental premises of Japan's foreign policy. Obviously, Japan's external strategy should be restructured in this new era, but what would be the core of Japan's new foreign policy and what could and should be done to pursue it? In order to find answers to this question, we decided that we needed to launch a research project that attempted to draw Japan's self-portrait in the post–Cold War era and identify its roles in the new world. More specifically, we were urged to identify a new foreign policy for Japan in the 1990s and to present the results as the policy proposal for the future.

Thus, Tadashi Yamamoto and JCIE launched a multiyear, interdisciplinary research project under the title "Japan's International Agenda." For this project, JCIE organized a team of seven well-known experts in specific foreign policy fields that were judged to be of highest importance. They were, in the economic realm, external trade strategy and

policy (Kazumasa Iwata), macroeconomic policy (Takatoshi Ito), structural adjustments (Heizo Takenaka), and economic cooperation and
other financial flows to developing countries (Makoto Sakurai); and in
the political/security realm, security strategy and policy (Akihiko Tanaka), relations with socialists countries (Yutaka Akino), and international implications of science and technology policy (Taizo Yakushiji). I
was designated to lead this powerful team, a pleasant and stimulating
but nevertheless challenging job for a generalist like me, and to contribute an introductory chapter integrating the findings and insights of team
members. Choices of individual topics were admittedly heavily affected
by our concerns about U.S.–Japan relations. Indeed, it can be said that
underlying this project was an urge to respond intelligently to criticism
of Japan by so-called revisionists, particularly those advocating the view
that Japan is inherently different from the rest of the world and thus has
to be contained.

The team met several times at various stages of the project and made
two trips to the United States to test ideas on scholars, researchers,
journalists, congressional staff, and other intellectuals in the United
States. Similar efforts were also made at other JCIE-sponsored intellectual dialogues such as the (U.S.–Japan) Shimoda Conference, the Euro-
Japan Conference, and the ASEAN-Japan Dialogue. Eight papers had
been more or less completed by November 1991, but were then updated
and revised to adjust to the rapidly changing international environment
since late 1991. However, the changes in the socialist world, particularly
in the former Soviet Union, were so drastic and sweeping that we had to
drop Yutaka Akino's excellent paper on that part of the world.

Aside from the substance, the significance of this policy research
project lies in the fact that it was launched by a private, independent,
nonprofit institution. In Japan, public policy-making has long been mo-
nopolized by the bureaucracy. Political parties and legislators have simply not been equipped with the necessary resources to engage in serious
policy formulation. Most private "think tanks," unlike their American
counterparts, are too busy following the guidelines established by the
companies or agencies to which they are attached to deliver independent
and timely policy proposals of their own. Japanese academia, on the
other hand, has tended to confine itself in the ivory tower and to look
down on policy-oriented studies as something demeaning to academic
inquiry. Journalists have traditionally opted to place themselves outside

the policy-making circle to retain their objectivity in covering the government. Such aversion to the policy-making process has severely crippled the private sector's ability to present alternatives to the governmental policies. This project, thus, was also an attempt to formulate an alternative for Japan's foreign policy, an act that is hopefully to be followed by many similar attempts.

In making specific policy proposals, members of the team were well aware of the numerous domestic obstacles standing in the way of implementation, obstacles described in the papers that follow. We are by no means optimists concerning the pertinacity of these domestic constraints. However, when one tackles such a major issue as a nation's foreign policy, particularly when one desires to change its direction, one must retain some level of optimism. And, in the course of deliberation, the team came to share a cautiously optimistic outlook on these constraints. We came to believe that Japan could change and that our work could make a difference.

I would like to take this opportunity to express my utmost gratitude to Tadashi Yamamoto, without whose encouragement, organization, and intellectual guidance neither the Japan's International Agenda project nor this volume would exist. I have always been an admirer of his insights and contribution as a genuine "intellectual entrepreneur." Words of thanks are also in order for Yamamoto's competent staff, including Hideko Katsumata, Hiroshi Peter Kamura, and Makito Noda, who successfully coordinated this challenging project. The project was made possible through generous grants from the John D. and Catherine T. MacArthur Foundation and Masahide Shibusawa of Tokyo's East-West Seminar. Shibusawa also actively participated in the team's discussions and hosted one of the team's meetings at his Asia Center in Odawara. Last, we are very grateful to our American, European, and Asian friends who took time to read our papers and took part in our discussion.

Introduction: Japan's International Agenda for the 1990s

Yoichi Funabashi

Japan has increasingly become an enigma to the rest of the world because of a variety of seeming inconsistencies. Japan is unquestionably an economic and technological superpower. But it remains an immature political player, keeping a low profile in world politics: Japan has often been described as having a first-class economy with "economy class" politics. Even within its economy a gap exists between the world-class competitiveness of many of its industries and the humble living standards of the ordinary Japanese. As a result, Japan may appear paramount and strong from one angle, but it may seem weak and small from another. In short, Japan is difficult to fathom. Ever since it debuted on the international scene when it defeated powerful, imperial Russia at the beginning of the twentieth century, Japan has seemed headed toward becoming a superpower quite unlike other nations that have achieved that status. In other words, Japan appears heretical.

One of Japan's priority tasks is, thus, to try to fill these gaps. In fact, efforts have already started, among which the legislation of a bill enabling the dispatch of noncombatant Self-Defense Forces to assist in the United Nations Peace Keeping Operation (UNPKO) activities in Cambodia and the proposed visit to China by Emperor Akihito merit special attention because they directly address the weakest points in

1

Japanese foreign policy: the first can be interpreted as an impoitant step toward Japan's larger presence and gicater weight in the United Nations; the lottei decision was taken in order to overcome its Asian neighbors' mistrust of Japan.

Nevertheless, these steps have just begun and they have yet to reflect national consensus. In fact, Japanese public opinion has been split and adrift. Japan is clearly at a crossroads. The most outstanding evidence of this was seen during the Gulf Crisis of 1990.

1. Crisis

A crisis almost always reveals the real picture. The Gulf Crisis revealed the real Japan. In the moment of truth, an economic superpower found itself merely an automatic teller machine, albeit one that needs a couple of kicks before it dishes out the money. The notion that economic power inevitably translates into geopolitical influence is a materialist illusion. So argued Charles Krauthammer,[1] and many Japanese now seem to subscribe to the view.

The Gulf Crisis was the manifestation of the failure of Japan's leadership. When the crisis erupted, Japan had its politically weakest leadership of the postwar era. The slow and cumbersome decision-making procedures benefited the powerful bureaucracies and served the status quo but was totally unfit to respond quickly in a crisis.

In 1989 Japan's ruling party, the Liberal Democratic party (LDP), had lost control in the Upper House, and now it encountered great difficulty in forming a coalition with the opposition parties, the Democratic Social party and the Komeito, on its response to the Gulf Crisis. The public was polarized. Japan had not witnessed such a divergence of views on a vital issue of this magnitude in thirty years.

Certainly Japan managed to be a part of the international coalition effort with its 13 billion dollar contribution. But it could not meaningfully make a "human resource" contribution on even a negligible scale and fell short even of Korea's dispatch of 150 medics and the Philippines' contribution of 190 doctors and nurses.

In sum, the Gulf Crisis demonstrated the enormous gap between Japan's economic might and its immature political prowess and still-low level of real internationalization.

There are many Japanese who are happier now because the national consensus was clearly solidified against sending troops abroad. Many feel that Japan did what it could and that we, as well as the foreigners, should not expect too much of Japan. Moreover, the 13 billion dollars, made possible only by a tax increase, was not peanuts. It was more than Japan's Official Development Assistance (ODA) in 1991, approximately $11 billion, which was the largest ODA disbursement by a single country in 1991.

Besides that, the Gulf War and its crisis management perhaps should not be viewed as a future pattern but rather as a unique phenomenon. A "new world order" should not take for granted the way the Gulf Crisis was settled and the way the coalition strategy worked.

However, the Gulf Crisis and War crystallized and magnified the issues that Japan should have addressed long ago, but did not. To Japan, the Gulf Crisis was, in a way, the day of reckoning.

The price of success has suddenly started to confront Japan exactly at the juncture when Japan's economic success has reached its peak. Japan's aggressive economic expansion has met strong resistance in both the United States and Western Europe. Japan's chronic trade surplus has been a constant political irritant to them throughout the 1980s. Japan's massive foreign investments have caused protectionist responses, particularly in the United States. The rare situation in which the world's largest debtor, the United States, militarily protects the world's largest creditor, Japan, has strained their relationship and the world system. Japan's rapid emergence as a political military power with highly sophisticated dual-use technologies has made some of the military planners in the major powers uneasy, especially in the United States. A group of revisionists has argued that Japan's specialness—its unique socioeconomic structure—is a destabilizing factor in the world system and has proposed that Japan should be treated separately.

At the same time, the political stability that has helped Japan achieve its economic goals in the past suddenly seems shaky. The dominance of the opposition parties in the Upper House election and generational change within the ruling Liberal Democratic party cloud the future. Nationalistic sentiments suppressed since World War II, generated partly by economic self-confidence and partly by frustration with mounting pressures from abroad, now surface more visibly. The deep-rooted pacifist tendencies of the public in Japan has increasingly constrained Japan's global and regional engagements.

The Gulf Crisis broke out exactly when the gap between Japan's underdeveloped political capacity to sustain a dream of a new global power and its seemingly uncontrollable expansion of economic power was most pronounced. The outcome was a shocking experience, rudely awakening Japan to its inability to cope with a crisis affecting its vital interests.

The international environment in the 1990s will no longer allow Japan to follow a one-dimensional economic strategy. The call for Japan to bear a full share of the burden to sustain the world system has intensified, and Japan knows that it must increase its share. However, the essential question is, for what purpose should Japan assume a larger share of the burden? Japan must clearly define its objectives and its role in the world rather than just respond to the call quantitatively. This will severely challenge Japan's long-standing set of strategic premises and policy foundations.

2. Japan's Past Strategy

Japan's self-image as a small, strategically naked and economically fragile island nation has changed as it has gradually become a respected member of the world community. Japan's inclusion as a founding member of the Group of Seven (G-7) economic summit in 1975 helped transform the Japanese public's perception of its own country. A decade later, the image of economic power was replaced by that of economic superpower as Japan suddenly found itself the world's largest creditor nation. With the collapse of the Warsaw Pact and the end of the Cold War, a new perception of Japan as a global economic power will be more widespread as the world becomes more polycentric.

Ironically, as Japan's international power has advanced since the 1980s, the underpinnings of its political and economic systems and conditions have been questioned. Japan's rapidly aging population, unique lifelong employment system, homogeneous social fabric, "plutocratic collusion" among leading industries, speculative "bubbles and bursts" in financial markets, and its complacency have been pinpointed as vulnerabilities or signs of decline. The sun, it is now declared, also sets, and the immobility of Japan's political leadership and system will accelerate the decline.

It is, however, too early to deliver a verdict on Japan's decline.

Contrary to the arguments of some revisionists, Japan has a proven capacity to adapt to new international environments, as in the cases of the Meiji Restoration and the rebuilding of the nation after World War II.

Nonetheless, Japan's strategic premises are still basically conditioned by a historical sense of vulnerability. They are the legacies of traumatic defeat and determination to be born again. These legacies are many, yet the following stand out: adaptation and catch-up, concentration on economic gains, following the lead of the United States, and restraint of regional strategy.

1. Adaptation and Catch-Up

Throughout its modern history, Japan has geographically and historically felt secluded from the world. The sharpened sense of "latecomer" and "odd man out" in the world scene has contributed to Japan's familiar foreign policy behavior of both inward-looking exceptionalism (ultranationalism in prewar days and pacifism in the postwar era) and desperate effort to catch up to the advanced nations (rectification of unequal treaties in the Meiji period and "GNPism" after World War II).

Deeply confined by this mindset, Japan has seldom tried to present itself as a rule maker in the world community. The rules were already there, and Japan simply tried to adapt itself to them and, if possible, to excel in playing the game—although, when faced with difficulty, it just tended to ignore and reject.

In general, Japan has long regarded the international environment as something to which it must adjust whenever a new situation arises. To Japan, the world order is a given and Japan is a reactor par excellence. In one Japanese political scientist's words, to Japan, "the world is nothing but a 'framework' or the setting which can change only mysteriously."[2] Prime Minister Takeo Fukuda's "equidistance diplomacy" in large part reflected the psychological block against defining the priorities of the foreign policy.

Japan's apparent obsession with the stratification and ranking of its status in the world also testified to its lack of will to define its self-image and role in the world. Economism or "GNPism" was a strategy to eschew political involvement. Prime Minister Zenko Suzuki's introduction of the theme of Japan as the "10 percent nation" *(ichiwari kokka)*—

a nation occupying 10 percent of world GNP—and his call for his fellow citizens to make a greater international contribution revealed that Japan perceived the world and its status in quantitative terms. Japan conspicuously avoided determining its self-image and role in qualitative terms.

Japan's former vice-minister for foreign affairs, Takakazu Kuriyama, lately argued for Japan's new diplomatic posture by coining the phrase, "foreign policy of a major power with an unassuming posture." Yet, this thrust for a new posture was expressed by attitudinal concepts rather than strategic ones.

Shintaro Ishihara's much-publicized book—perhaps the best seller worldwide written by a Japanese in the late 1980s—merely worsened the situation for, as indicated by the title of the book, *Japan That Can Say No,* it was a rejection, not a projection, of a national psyche.

Japan's weight and stake in the world economy and world politics have increased the world's interest and stake in Japan's strategy and policy. The role gap between Japan's lack of projection and other countries' increasing expectations of Japan has widened to a precarious degree. Japan is now a part of a given order and must be an actor.

2. Concentration on Economic Gains

Japan's mercantile strategy since the last war was almost unanimously supported by the public and enthusiastically pushed forward for four decades. Japan's new determination, symbolized by the "Peace Constitution," was so strong that almost all the responses and energy were mobilized into economic reconstruction and expansion. Military and security issues were constantly put on the back burner. Noneconomic policy goals such as international peacekeeping and human rights were never vigorously pursued.

This exclusively economic-oriented strategy became increasingly untenable by the mid-1980s. First, the scale of the Japanese economy and its overseas penetration have caused political repercussions that forced Japan to respond politically. The voluntary restrictions on automobile exports to the United States throughout the 1980s was typical. Second, Japan's creditor status compelled it to endorse many international programs with strategic implications—a Latin American debt relief program, an East European recovery plan, Middle East peacekeeping, etc.—

and to change the nature of its economic diplomacy. At the same time, louder criticism of "checkbook diplomacy" is likely to be heard. Third, Japan's newly acquired and developed militarily relevant technology is transforming Japan into a country of increasing military significance. Japan's long-standing nonmilitary strategy has been based on the premise of being a "have-not" in terms of indigenous military resources. Now this premise is shaken because Japan clearly belongs to the club of "haves" due to its military-related technology.

3. Following the Lead of the United States

Throughout modern history, Japan benefited enormously from the liberal world economic system, whether the hegemonic power of the system was the Netherlands, Great Britain, or the United States. After absorbing advanced technology and goods from the Dutch via the state-sanctioned outpost off Nagasaki in the Edo period, Japan was prepared to modernize when most countries of the non-Western world were colonized by imperialistic powers. The Anglo-Japanese alliance during the first two decades of this century provided a security blanket for Japan that enabled it to overcome its deep-rooted fear of the threat from Russia. Rapid economic development and trade expansion, not surprisingly, coincided with the era.

The U.S.–Japan alliance in the postwar era provided both security and a market for Japanese products. Japan's economic miracle required U.S. protection. For many Japanese, the lessons are clear. Japan prospered when it followed the leadership of the world's most liberal economic power. Hence a strategy of following was born, cherished, and developed into almost an axiom.

The strategy has changed during the Nakasone era when Japan has tried to seek a higher profile and a broader role in world politics. Prime Minister Yasuhiro Nakasone's commitment to the Western alliance based on the assumption of global security as "indivisible" reflected Japan's search for leadership. Nakasone's high-yen strategy, which contributed to laying the ground for the Plaza Agreement in 1985, was tantamount to a declaration of Japan's new role as a world banker. Nakasone's policy change for fiscal expansion that he pledged at the Venice Summit in 1987 paved the way for Japan's new task as an "absorber" country—a market power. Yet the habit of Japan's leadership to see the world merely through the prism of U.S.–Japanese relations limits the scope of its foreign policy.

The deep-rooted hierarchical relationships in Japanese society often make it difficult for the Japanese to perceive and execute a more effective foreign policy because of their inability to assimilate the concept of equality in international relations. Japanese "dependencia" psychology—viewing America as a big brother—and its lack of initiative in effect invites *gaiatsu* (foreign pressure). Exploitation of foreign pressure in order to divert domestic attention away from unpopular policies is a strategy employed universally. It is frequently employed, particularly by the industrial democracies, in managing the ever-growing relations of economic interdependence. It has both positive and negative effects on the stability of international relationships. In Japan, it is a most habitually—and often unilaterally—used play because of its effectiveness in overcoming the immobility of the Japanese political system. The coining of an entirely new word, *gaiatsu,* to denote foreign pressure indicates the degree to which it has taken root in Japan's political culture.

However, this tactic causes problems.

First, the use of foreign pressure does not help generate healthy policy debates or create a good milieu in which to promote Japan's own initiative. It shifts debates away from the issue of what Japan should do in its own best interest and toward what other countries want Japan to do. For this very reason, it often arouses nationalistic feelings and emotionalizes the issues.

Second, it provides a "cover" for those who actually pursue their own agenda (e.g., sending Self-Defense Forces abroad) under the guise of policy coordination with others, particularly with the United States. Abused *gaiatsu* politics undermines the U.S.–Japan relationship because it tends to perpetuate the patron-protegé relationship and love-hate emotions between the two countries.

Overdependence on its bilateral relationship with the United States undermines Japan's creative diplomacy by closing off other avenues for foreign policy initiatives. The Gulf Crisis magnified the problem.

During the crisis, Japan felt left out from the core of the decision-making process of the coalition diplomacy. Japan is not a permanent member of the U.N. Security Council. It does not belong to a collective security body such as NATO, nor to regional and supranational organizations such as the European Community. The G-7 mechanism was not mobilized for coalition building among the trilateral countries. There was no urgent meeting among the G-7. Nor was any attempt made to coordinate policies among the political directors of the G-7. The only G-7 working vehicle was that of the finance ministers, and its mission was simply to write checks. Secretary of State James A. Baker III did not visit Japan. Lack of a sense of participation in and commitment to a legitimate decision-making body, although partly a result of Japan's constitutional and political constraints, lessened public support for a stronger commitment to a coalition strategy. Japan felt strategically naked again and thus was driven to further reliance on relations with the United States.

4. Restraint of Regional Strategy

The bankruptcy of the Greater East Asian Co-Prosperity Sphere resulted in a profound political and psychological inhibition, affecting Japan's postwar strategy. Whenever Japan tried to assert itself and assume leadership in the region, it was reminded of its guilt in the postwar era by repeated warnings from Asian leaders about Japan's "new ambition" and references to "a step toward becoming a military giant."

The lack of a regional cooperative economic and military framework in Asia and the Pacific region, such as NATO and the EEC, both of which helped West Germany overcome its constraints on regional strategy, handicapped Japan. The Japanese government's attempt to introduce a bill to enable Self-Defense Forces to be sent abroad for the purpose of contributing to the multinational forces in the Persian Gulf area in the fall of 1990 met suspicion and opposition in Asian countries that feared the possible consequences of Japan's power projection.

Japan's reluctance and resistance to formulating a regional strategy and the heavy dependence of its economic expansion on the United States and world trade have made Japan one of the few countries in the modern world with truly global interests.[3] Regionalism was regarded as a tainted word both politically and economically. It was bad politics and bad economics because it implied political domination by an ambitious hegemonic power and a bloc economy that threatened to destroy the free trading system. Japan's diversification of its export markets, especially its dependence on the U.S. market, unlike the concentration on Asian markets in prewar days, encouraged Japan to devote itself to engaging in the global but U.S.–led multilateral economic framework. Although Japan heavily concentrated its ODA on Asian neighbors— more than 60 percent of all aid money—it did not develop a comprehensive regional policy.

This does not mean, however, that Japan has not developed any regional policies. In fact, Japan has implemented a series of "new look" regional policies, including the establishment of formal diplomatic relations with Korea in 1965; the launching of ODA in 1969, partially in order to improve the resilience of the two-year old Association of Southeast Asian Nations (ASEAN); efforts to normalize diplomatic relations with China in view of Nixon's abrupt approach to Beijing; consolidation of ties with Asian oil producers after the two oil crises; and emphasis on "heart-to-heart" policies towards Asian countries proposed by Prime Minister Fukuda immediately following the fall of Saigon. But these policies never fully blossomed due to constraints imposed by Japan's negative wartime legacies in Asia, absence of a multilateral framework in the region, and two regional "hot wars" during the Cold War. At the same time, the United States also tried to encourage closer relations between Japan and its Asian neighbors, although it should be noted that the United States aimed to confine these relations within the larger framework of the Cold War.

The big steps forward toward a single market taken by the European Community and the United States–Canada Free Trade Agreement since the mid-1980s have forced Japan to reconsider its approach. European integration can be viewed as a classic "challenge and response" case. It was, in large part, driven by the challenge from the dynamic economies of Japan and other Asia-Pacific countries. Now Europe challenges Japan. A unified Germany as a solid nucleus for and East Europe as a new eastern frontier of a colossal Europe sharpen the sense of challenge. The prospects of United States–Canada economic integration by the end of the decade and a United States–Mexico Free Trade zone in the future also force Japan to entertain "new thinking" about the regional framework.

The aggressive bilateralism of U.S. trade policy, the prospect of U.S. military disengagement in the Asian-Pacific region, and the need to incorporate the People's Republic of China and the Soviet Union as responsible players in the region will encourage the momentum toward broad regional cooperation. In the multipolar world after the end of the

Cold War, a regional framework can provide some sort of "safety net" for each country.

However, the problem remains: How viable is Asian-Pacific regionalism, politically and economically? Can Japan assume leadership? How does Japan relate to the existing framework of the world system? There have emerged new orientations for and interests in Japan's regional strategy in recent years. Influential business leaders such as Yotaro Kobayashi argue for the need for Japan's re-Asianization. However, this may develop into an anti-Western, particularly anti-American feeling among Japanese.

Japan's modernization process has been like the swing of a pendulum, first swinging toward the West, then back to indigenous and culturally familiar Asia. Japan's soul-searching effort to define its proper self-image in the world and Asia is still haunted by legacies of past swings.

3. Japan's New Strategy

Japan's new international agenda for the 1990s must respond to a variety of new issues and challenges.

1. Global Civilian Power

Japan must establish its self-image in the world. It must express its cherished values and self-enlightened interests. Yet a new self-image projection should not be radical; rather, a conscious effort should be made to develop it incrementally. Japan's unorthodox power portfolio ("economic giant and military dwarf") should not be viewed as an unstable and transitional phenomenon. On the contrary, the portfolio's very nature gives Japan a golden opportunity to define its power and role in the radically changing world of the 1990s. The changing nature of power in the increasingly interdependent world will upgrade economic and technological capacity, educational quality, and the developmental model effect in which Japan excels.

The widespread perception that the Gulf War, after all, underscores the supremacy of military power as the ultimate power element should not alter Japan's new strategy of being a global civilian power.[4] Japan should search for various avenues of enhancing political power based on economic strength, not on military might, in order to stimulate a new perception of the changing nature of power in the world community and the recognition that Japan should be accepted as a prototype of the global civilian power.

It can be said that "global civilian power" is a concept of power that fits well with Japan's long-term national interests. If Japan's adoption of this concept is internationally accepted and if Japan thus can contribute to the "civilianization" of the international community, it could in turn contribute to the creation of the international environment that is favorable to Japan's national interests.

Japan's economic interests are global, and they require Japan's global commitment. Thus, Japan's power must be global in dimension. Secondly, it must be realized that Japan is fragile because it is a civilization that has blossomed in the Far Eastern offshore of the Urasian continent, strategically unprotected. Now that the threat from the North or the USSR has receded, and the prospects for effective U.N. operation are brighter for the first time, Japan has a better chance to develop itself into a civilian power. Furthermore, the time has arrived at which Japan's choice of the path toward civilian power may itself affect the security environments of the international community, particularly the Asian-Pacific region. Thirdly, adoption of the path to becoming a global civilian power will be a natural and long-lasting choice of the Japanese who had strongly supported the postwar peace strategy based on the, so to speak, second "sword hunt" after the first and authentic arms abduction implemented by Toyotomi Hideyoshi in the sixteenth century.

On the other hand, some questions are immediately raised regarding Japan's will to develop into a global civilian power: (1) Isn't civilianization of Japan (and Germany) possible only with the presence of a super-power, the United States? (2) Isn't the United Nations unlikely to be the lender of last resort in the international security system? (3) Will the burden-sharing work smoothly with countries that are willing to provide military contributions if a civilian power restricts its external military contribution, just as Japan had done during the economic sanction on Iraq? As indicated by these questions, the concept is still plagued with problems and uncertainty. But then what will be the alternative available to Japan? It may be an ordinary choice for a country of Japan's status to become a military power, but an important question is whether the United States will approve of Japan taking this ordinary path. In terms of its contribution to the United Nations, Japan should limit its security-related contributions to the level of the PKO and, instead, provide numerous nonmilitary contributions. The concept of security itself will develop into a more comprehensive one, including such nonmilitary elements as the environment, nonproliferation of nuclear arms and plutonium, and economic development, which will enable Japan to "demilitarize" its contribution to international security. Japan, then, can share a fair burden of international security as defined by this new concept.

Japan's constitution was a blessing to the Japanese not only because it has remained the underpinning of Japan's postwar democratic institutions but also because it was imbued with universal values. The constitution itself was a descendant of the "new thinking" reflected in Franklin Roosevelt's "four freedoms," the Atlantic Charter, and the United Nations Charter.

The meanings and lessons of the "Peace Constitution" and Hiroshima should be universally shared. Japan has a special obligation to make these meanings and lessons not slogans but a legitimate common heritage of humankind by ensuring that they are relevant and palatable to other people and countries.

Japan must pursue two psychologically conflicting mindsets and styles—active engagement in world peace and self-restraint as a military power. Japan can and should overcome its uncertainty over its image and role in the world community. Japan should push forward along the path of a global civilian power with its interests reaching well beyond its regional confines, while its military posture is limited to the self-defense of its islands.

2. Multiple Value-Oriented Diplomacy

Japan's one-dimensional economic strategy must be replaced by a multiple value-oriented strategy. It is high time for the world banker to design and contribute to the building of an international order based upon something more than economic growth. In particular, four values should be given much higher priority as goals of Japan's international strategy: the effort to be a model for poorer countries and to give them assistance for their economic development and their gradual promotion of democratic values, peacekeeping, promotion of human rights, and promotion of environmental protection.

In the 1990s, for the first time in its modern history, Japan will be substantially free from security threats from the North, whether they be explicit or latent, ideological and/or military. Although the post–Cold War world surely will see many smaller-scale and regional conflicts, and even wars, such as that in the Persian Gulf, the Asian-Pacific area may have a better chance to maintain peace than in the turbulent days of the 1940s (Pacific War), the 1950s (Korean War), or the 1960s (Vietnam War).

Global interdependence and a higher priority for the economic dimension in statecraft benefit Japan in the sense that they suit Japan's peace strategy and enhance its means through financial and economic resources. Japan should take advantage of this and mobilize its resources to pursue a broader set of goals aimed at promoting a compatible world order.

As the East-West conflict is receding rapidly, the North-South conflict is likely to be intensified in the 1990s. Japan's experience, together with that of the Asian NIEs (Newly Industrializing Economies), will help poorer countries develop their economies. Japan should multiply its effort to transfer its technical and financial expertise to these countries so that it will strengthen their economic foundations and stabilize their political superstructures.

Japan's commitment to peace, embodied and enshrined in its "Peace Constitution" and subsequent policies, should be given a wider context within which they can be more fully recognized internationally and can simultaneously contribute to multilateral peacekeeping.

As for human rights, Japan has been reluctant to place this issue on its foreign policy agenda. The reasons for this vary. Japan's foreign policy-making is not usually under heavy pressure from moralistic grass-roots movements. The dependence of Japan's economy on conservative and feudalistic Saudi Arabia and its sensitive relationship with China and the Republic of Korea force Japan to think twice before speaking up on human rights. Japan's sense of guilt after World War II toward neighboring countries, especially China and Korea, puts a psychological brake on criticizing human rights violations and exerting diplomatic pressure. Human rights is somehow regarded as a "luxury" of such countries as the United States and France, which were lucky enough to claim moral superiority because of victory in the war.

These constraints will not disappear easily. However, Japan should reconsider them and take a more active stance on human rights in foreign policy. Protecting human rights will be more crucial to peacekeeping among nations as the world will likely face more ethnic and nationalistic conflicts in the 1990s. Ensuring that the rights of minorities are respected and internationally monitored is the most effective way to prevent violations and reduce the chances of conflict.

Japan recently began to explore ways to set some political conditions on its economic aid policy. The government of Japan explains that four criteria—level of military expenditure, potential of atomic, biological, and chemical (ABC) weapons and missiles, arms trade, and democratization—are supposed to be taken into consideration in future ODA. The new approach, although its effectiveness still remains to be seen, clearly reflects the stronger yearnings and demands of Japan's public for human rights.

An extremely delicate case concerns Japan's relationship with China, as Japan's tortured diplomacy after the Tiananmen incident demonstrated. Although Japan cannot and must not moralize about its foreign policy and must be mindful of its strategic relationship with China, Japan can more effectively convey its advice and remind the Chinese authorities, as well as the Chinese people, of Japan's aspirations for human rights. Otherwise, Japan's relationship with China will be viewed more as collusion between the apparatchiks of both ruling parties and pursuit of single-minded economic interests both in Japan and abroad. This view would eventually undermine the value of the relationship as the Japanese and Chinese people will regard it more negatively.

Japan also has minority groups, although they are relatively small. Japan's human rights diplomacy, first and foremost, should be directed toward its own minorities, particularly the Korean community of some six hundred thousand persons, to enhance their status and political and economic rights. However, this is not enough. Japan should put more emphasis on human rights and democratic values as goals of its foreign policy and as a legitimate expression of the aspirations of its people. With the fiftieth anniversary of the end of World War II approaching, it is desirable that Japan hasten the completion of its round of rectification of wartime vices. The proposed emperor's trip to China and the imminent visit to Korea must provide Japan with opportunities to squarely face its past, admit and apologize for its past evils, and offer compensations where necessary. These acts will then mark the beginning of a new era when the framework of genuine peace and stability can be constructed. At the same time, Japan should promote joint studies on contemporary history with experts from neighboring Asian countries, encourage the joint authorship of history textbooks, and improve the quality of history education based on findings from these joint works.

Japan's expression of values in foreign policy must be matched by more strenuous efforts to make its own political system more democratic, and its own economic structure more open and liberal, so as to make its institutions and practices more compatible with like-minded democracies.

3. Full Partnership and Supportive Leadership

Japan lacks institutions through which it can pursue its policies. This constraint needs to be overcome.

Japan should search for various avenues of enhancing political power based on economic might, not on military power, in order to stimulate a new perception of the changing nature of power and the recognition that Japan, in these new terms, is a power in its own right. Japan should be allowed to maintain the role of a global civilian power and a full partner with the other major powers in a polycentric world.

Japan should initiate a much fuller partnership with the United States from a global perspective. Japan's "global partnership" with the United States—a new look designed in the meeting between President George Bush and Prime Minister Toshiki Kaifu in the spring of 1990—proved to be a nonstarter only several months later. Yet the concept should be defined and developed as Japan evolves into a more mature partner.

However, the Japanese should not believe that this means equal standing with the United States. It is not necessary or desirable for Japan to try to obtain such standing. Over the next decade, Japan's relationship with the United States as well as its role can be defined in terms of "supportive leadership." Its leadership role should not be principal but should instead be supportive of U.S. global posture and commitment.

The United States will be the sole superpower in the 1990s. Because of its superior military resources and logistics, it will probably be the only country with the capacity to be the equivalent of the "lender of the last resort" in providing a security blanket in a military crisis.

Although some argue that the Gulf War demonstrated the return of an American unipolar system, it can be safely argued that it demonstrated the need for the United States to exert its leadership in a coalition effort. But the Gulf Crisis is only one example of a threat that will confront the world in the future. Even a confident United States will not always be able to cope with a diversity of threats by itself.

First, it will be, at least in the foreseeable future, subject to financial limitations. Second, the United States will have to pay more attention to a wider range of issues besides security matters, such as its economy, the environment, human rights, and drugs. These issues will pose problems for the traditional pattern of U.S. hegemonic leadership because they require collective leadership and policy coordination. Third, the United States will gradually disengage militarily from Europe and the Asian-Pacific region and is likely to face inward-looking and even isolationist sentiments and political forces in the future.

It is for these reasons that Japan can and should augment and complement U.S. leadership. Japan can buttress U.S. leadership with financial resources, at least in the next decade. Japan can play a leading role in the coordination of macroeconomic policies, economic aid, environmental protection, and high-technology development. More specifically, Japan's major task in providing supportive leadership is to stimulate U.S. interests in the global open-trade system and manage the dollar so that the United States overcomes its twin deficits while maintaining noninflationary economic growth. Japan also has an absorber function, principally for neighboring Asian-Pacific countries, in reducing the U.S. external trade imbalance and lessening the burden on the United States.

Japan's supportive leadership should not be viewed as a matter of simply following the United States nor of financially underwriting U.S. military actions. Instead, Japan should be regarded as a provider of collective goods indispensable in the age of collective leadership.

As the Gulf Crisis reminded us of emotional resentment on both sides, with its perceptions of "rent-a-cop" versus "automatic teller machine," it is imperative for both sides to define mutually compatible and respectable roles in pursuing common goals. Accordingly, the style and pattern of exerting leadership should be managed in a new fashion. Japan should share decision-making on crucial global matters as a full partner and should make its own major decisions in consultation with the United States to ensure that their directions and priorities are harmonious. It is most critical for both countries to constantly search for mutually compatible policies vis-à-vis the Soviet Union and China, perhaps the two most unstable big powers in the 1990s.

The U.S.–Japan security alliance should continue to be the underpinning of a dynamic and sound bilateral relationship and an anchor of Asian-Pacific security in the foreseeable future. Japan's alliance with the United States is the third alliance that Japan has forged in its modern history. However, unlike the Anglo-Japanese alliance in the early days of the century and the Axis alliance with Germany and Italy in prewar days, the U.S.–Japan alliance was not a mere invention of realpolitik but a far more pervasive engagement and a symbol of friendship and stability between two societies. It can continue to function as such and be a stabilizing factor in the Asian-Pacific peace structure. At the same time, Japan's excessive bilateral foreign policy orientation should be better balanced by strengthening multilateral (United Nations, General Agreement on Tariffs and Trade [GATT]), trilateral, and regional diplomacies: As more constraints will be put on U.S. leadership and the need for policy coordination becomes stronger in the future, a search for wider options and alternatives will be necessary. Japan's contribution to this task is the essence of supportive leadership.

4. Pacific Globalism

Japan must not delude itself into believing that its identity can be developed in purely regional terms, its economy sustained in the Asian bloc, and its political ambitions fulfilled in integration in the area.

Yet, Japan must have its regional strategy. Its region must not be confined to Asia, particularly East Asia, but must be widened to encompass the Asian-Pacific rim, including the United States. Its objective is to keep the region open, peaceful, and democratic. Regionalism thus understood can be called "Pacific globalism."

In the coming years, Japan's strategy for Pacific globalism consists of three pillars:

1. To promote economic growth and development as well as liberalize and multilateralize trade and investment in the region.
2. To enhance the peacekeeping and peace-building mechanism and measures in the region by maximizing U.S. commitment and engagement.
3. To incorporate the rapidly changing Socialist countries (the Soviet Union, China, Vietnam, and North Korea) into the region as responsible players in the region.

As for economic liberalization in the region, Japan can sustain and reinvigorate U.S. global interests and posture by infusing the emerging Pacific globalism (e.g., a new and strong interest in propelling the Uruguay Round of the Asia-Pacific Economic Cooperation [APEC] countries) into the aging Atlanticist globalism in place since the days of the Atlantic Charter.

By doing so, Japan can play a constructive role in deterring European and North American regionalism from becoming exclusivist and can create a favorable milieu in which to integrate the Soviet Union and China into the region. It also can help mitigate the thrusts toward inward-looking and nationalistic action in Asian countries as well as the call for a restrictive and close regional grouping.

In the realm of security, Japan is constrained from playing a leading role and is likely to retain those constraints in the 1990s. The United States still will be required to play the leading role as the stabilizing country in the region, and its bilateral alliance with some countries in the region, particularly Japan and Australia, will be the anchor of the security framework. Japan's role will be to support the anchor. But it should think of that role in terms of contributing to broader regional security rather than Japan's security alone.

The countries in the Asian region should discuss security matters with each other more directly. Three elements—the United States, the reinvigorated United Nations, and the countries in the region—are indispensable to fostering a better security climate in Asia.

The problem for Japan's regional strategy lies in Japan itself. Japan's reluctance to face up to the past colonization of Korea, invasion of China, domination over Southeast Asia, and guilt for war crimes—and its feeble effort to educate or reeducate its people about true history—generate a deep suspicion and mistrust all over Asia. Reluctance also creates complacent and self-indulgent views of Japan's own history among the Japanese. New currents of nationalistic feeling, though still amorphous and undefined, may gather momentum and run a dangerous course if not checked and redressed by studies of and education about the historic facts. The perception that Japan has not come to terms with its own past constitutes the fundamental constraint on an effective and successful foreign policy.

Ironically, Japan's strong pacifist tendencies in the Gulf Crisis simultaneously relieved and worried some neighboring countries. They were relieved that Japan resisted military projection abroad and worried because of its isolationist dangers. Some Southeast Asian countries, notably Thailand and Malaysia, now seem to be more relaxed about accepting Japan's political leadership in the region, while Northeast Asia, China, and Korea still are alarmed by the prospect. Nonetheless, the perception of Japan and its leadership is subtly changing in the region. It is crucial for Japan to face up to the past and educate its own citizens about its modern history if it wants to pursue a viable regional strategy.

4. Issues in the 1990s

In the 1990s, Japan's relationship with the Soviet Union (and the Russian Republic) may be normalized due to a possible settlement of the unresolved Northern Territory issue. It may well be that economic development in Siberia and the Pacific Maritime Provinces will gain momentum with the infusion of Japan's capital and technology. It is highly advisable that reduction of military capability in the region be promoted by the concerned parties (the United States, the Soviet Union, Japan, China, South Korea, North Korea, and Canada) in tandem with multinational development projects.

The search for a peace structure in the Northeast Asian region should not copy the Conference on Security and Cooperation of Europe (CSCE) mechanism. The security environment and political configuration of Asia are different from those of Europe. In Asia, particularly Northeast Asia, it is more realistic to build multilayered security regimes. Confidence-building measures (CBMs) should be introduced on the Korean peninsula under the auspices of the Asian "two-plus-four" (North and South Korea, the United States, the Soviet Union, China, and Japan). Formalization of Korea-China diplomatic relations in the summer of 1992 reflects the accelerated changes in the East Asian Cold War regime, and this will positively affect the realization of "two-plus-four" negotiations. At the same time, a trilateral security dialogue among Japan, Korea, and the United States has become necessary in order to insure that these changes will not abruptly change the Far Eastern security framework based on security treaties between the United States and Korea and between the United States and Japan. We should think of first establishing a private consultative body among these three countries. The Northern Territory areas should be demilitarized along with the introduction of a free economic zone in the maritime provinces of the Soviet Union and a free port at Vladivostok. The U.S. naval nuclear offensive capability and presence should be reduced in proportion to the reduction of Soviet land nuclear arsenals and logistics. Normalization of Russo-Japanese relations should be hastened, as it is the prerequisite for Russia's growth to a stabilizing force in the region. It is also a prerequisite for the preparation of a stable structure for "two-plus-four" arrangements for the Korean peninsula. The unresolved territorial dispute between Russia and Japan may present a good excuse for a third power interfering in this bilateral issue.

With regard to China, Japan and the United States should regard it as a regional power and encourage it to be involved in Asian-Pacific economic expansion. There may emerge a new political force in China such as "a new authoritarian school" arguing that China should join Japan to oppose the "human rights imperialism of the United States." There is also a deep-rooted cultural and psychological affinity toward China in Japan that may take political shape, helped by mounting frustration with Japan-bashing by the United States. However, Japan should refrain from trying to establish an exclusive special relationship with China.

The "Peace Constitution" and subsequent commitments to peace should be not only vigorously maintained but also translated into a stimulant for multilateral peacekeeping.

Japan's commitment to the United Nations should be enhanced. As the Gulf Crisis demonstrated, Japan's legal and political preparedness for this sort of crisis is totally inadequate. Although the spirit and commitment of the "Peace Constitution," which prohibit Japan from sending military forces abroad, must be respected, Japan must be a much more active member of the United Nations and must make its nonmilitary resources available to the peacekeeping efforts of the United Nations. It is desirable that Japan be granted permanent member status in the Security Council. However, it is more advisable that it should develop some informal link between the Perm-5 and the G-7 to provide these groups with the perspectives and interests of Germany, Japan, and the European Community in the near future.

Japan's PKO cooperation must be implemented strictly under the auspices of the United Nations. It might be worthwhile to consider establishing "joint PKO forces" with other Asian countries under U.N. auspices. Someday, joint China-Japan PKO or Korea-Japan PKO may contribute to the elimination of mutual distrust between and among these countries.

The burden sharing and responsibility sharing should be put at the top of the agenda for policy coordination among trilateral countries as the world moves into an age of coalition management. Although it should not develop into a mechanical formula, there should be mutual understanding as to what constitutes fair contributions of each to the effort.

Japan should reconsider its aid policy to reflect its new course in multiple value-oriented diplomacy. Special attention should be paid to the peacekeeping efforts of each recipient country.

Japan should more actively lead in the effort against proliferation of nuclear and offensive conventional weapons and technologies by committing itself to its long-established principles and calling for similar commitments from other countries. Japan should express its aspirations in its aid policy, particularly to its neighboring countries, China and North Korea, two arms suppliers to the Middle East. Japan's normalization of relations with and economic aid to North Korea should be based on the premise that North Korea accept surveillance by the International Atomic Energy Agency (IAEA) and commit itself firmly not to develop nuclear weapons.

As for global environmental issues, Japan should commit itself to drastic cuts of carbon dioxide by the end of the century. The ODA devoted to environmental protection in recipient countries should be separately managed from ordinary ODA and should be given more flexible treatment for multiyear disbursement commitment and political considerations.

Regarding economic policy, Japan's agenda for the 1990s should have three pillars: promotion of a liberal world trading system beyond the Uruguay Round; tripod currency management system (dollar, yen, and ECU [European Currency Unit]), along with macroeconomic policy coordination of the G-7; and Asian-Pacific regional economic development.

Japan's new role under the new circumstances should be one of complementarity building—an effort to complement each of the multilateral, trilateral, and regional trade and economic arrangements in pursuit of a more open and stable global economy. On each level, Japan should take the lead to invigorate the mechanism. Japan should promote the Uruguay Round and push forward the creation of a Multilateral Trade Organization (MTO). Japan should also promote the Free Trade and Investment Agreement (FTIA) among Organization for Economic

Cooperation and Development (OECD) countries. It should engage in the multilateral Structural Impediments Initiative (SII) with the United States and Western Europe, preferably within the framework of the OECD, and set in motion a new process of coordination between macroeconomic and microeconomic policies in the G-7. Japan should, in cooperation with the United States and Western Europe, engage more fully in a surveillance and indicator mechanism to manage a more stable currency relationship among the dollar, yen, and ECU. It will be crucial for the three countries to intensify their efforts to promote cooperation for political and strategic reasons, too.

Concerning regionalism, Japan should contribute to enhancing the APEC by liberalizing its trade and economic systems and maintaining vigorous domestic demand. The APEC, still embryonic and lacking cohesion, should gradually be transformed into a policy-coordinating body so that at a certain point in the future its annual meetings can be held on a head-of-state level and timed prior to the G-7 annual summit. Japan, with the United States and Canada, can then represent its interests and deliver its message at the summit. When the APEC matures, it is worthwhile to explore the possibility of the head of the APEC Secretariat attending the G-7 summits in a fashion similar to representation of the EC. The U.S. presence and contribution is essential in the formation of any Asian-Pacific regional arrangement. Thus Japan should resist the call for an East Asian Economic Grouping (EAEG) by Prime Minister Mahathir of Malaysia, due to its exclusivity to the East Asian region.

Japan's leadership for more open economic systems must be rooted in its own market liberalization. The SII talks target politically sensitive sectors such as banking, securities, distribution, transportation, and construction industries, which have more or less remained untouched by the liberalization process in the past three decades. The SII implementation process will help lay the foundation for harmonization of Japan's economic and social system by gradually breaking up the iron triangle of vested interests. By setting an example in remedying its noncompetitive structure, Japan should urge other trading partners to do likewise.

5. Political Constraints

In the 1990s, two taboos of liberalization, opening the rice market and admitting an orderly infusion of foreign workers, at last will be broken. The political implications of rice-market liberalization and introduction of foreign workers will be so enormous that they will force a change in Japan's outdated electoral system and life-long employment system. The rice market has been treated as a "sanctuary." The powerful agricultural cooperative lobby has mounted tremendous pressure on politicians to protect the rice market. In the general election of early 1990, all the major political parties put up campaign banners about not letting "a grain of rice" into Japan. This may prove to be the last gasp of Japan's most protectionist forces.

Opening the rice market will correct the underrepresentation of metropolitan politicians and result in more balanced representation. Rice liberalization and electoral reform may be the historic equivalent of the repeal of the British Corn Law and the electoral revision of the mid–nineteenth century in the sense that liberalization will encourage liberal domestic constituents to sustain a more open trade and economic strategy.

The life-long employment system, already under stress in the face of a massive influx of part-time workers, a rapidly aging work force, and diversification of the company businesses will be fundamentally shaken by the influx of foreign workers. It will let loose the regimented and hierarchical structure of the "company standard" society and will harmonize uniquely Japanese management into a more internationally compatible style. In both cases, the psychological and political impacts will be far reaching.

Nevertheless, Japan is handicapped by its own political constraints on an effective and dynamic foreign policy. As was already pointed out, some political constraints on Japan's foreign policy-making and global leadership stood out during the Gulf Crisis—lack of initiative in developing new policies, lack of global institutions with which Japan can associate in effectively pursuing its policies, lack of acceptance of its leadership from its neighbors, and lack of recognition and realization of its unique power portfolio and desirable responsibility sharing.

Japan must examine its own political system and decision-making structure to overcome these constraints. The behavioral patterns and attitudes of Japanese society clash with the need for quick and dynamic formulation and implementation of foreign policy. The structural weakness of the leadership, highly personalized political allegiances and relationships among factions and parties, and the dominance of pork barrel politics all constitute characteristics of Japan's political culture and limit and restrain the outward projection of new aspirations and policies. The gap also may be a destabilizing factor in world financial markets in the future. The inability of Japan's leadership to cope with the unrealistically high price of land and stocks, for instance, has already caused a dangerous bubble, and a burst, in Japanese financial markets and thereby put a grave strain on Japan's macroeconomic policies.

Japan's consumers, particularly urban dwellers, increasingly find a gap between Japan's economic wealth and the quality of their standard of living, which sharpens their political awareness. In addressing this gap, Japan's bureaucrats and politicians have become problems rather than problem solvers. The bureaucracy and its symbiotic "policy tribes" in the LDP have formed "iron triangles" with protected industries to resist fundamental economic and social reforms.

It was joked in Japan during the SII talks that the loyal opposition was now in Washington, D.C., or that President Bush acted as chief of the LDP's largest faction. This disturbingly catches the mood of deep public frustration over the inability of the bureaucracy and political parties to act without outside pressure from the United States.

The immobility of Japan's decision-making process is exemplified well by the ubiquitous *gaiatsu* politics in Japan, which helps keep the existing political order in place by blaming foreigners (often, Washington) for uncomfortable accommodations. Reliance on *gaiatsu* is essentially a function of overcoming the immobility of the Japanese system. And this immobility is a product of institutional and cultural factors that include a bottom-to-top, consensus-oriented decision-making process, the supremacy of "domesticists" over internationalists, and the manner in which domestic political institutions must achieve mutual parity in burden sharing.

Japan cannot develop an effective international role until there is a significant measure of domestic political change.

First, Japan has only one political party capable of ruling. There is not yet a viable two-party or multiparty system. When the voters are especially unhappy with the government, they will in protest vote for the opposition, but many of these voters say that their purpose is to humble the LDP rather than to vote it out of office. The opposition has not yet developed the psychology and the policy positions required of a governing party. The quasi-coalition among the LDP, the Democratic Socialist party, and Komeito during the Gulf Crisis was a telling example of political immaturity. Nevertheless, the initiative for change must come from politicians, not from the bureaucrats. They must press for long-overdue political and electoral reform so as to assure fairer representation of the "silent majority" in big-city constituencies—a huge bloc of voters with a keener awareness of Japan's enlightened self-interest—in the political decision-making and voting processes. Politicians must start lively and constructive policy debates that will enhance the ability to develop meaningful policy proposals not dependent on the bureaucracy. They will have a better chance of doing so in the coming years now that the ideological overtones of the security issue—characteristic of the Diet debates in Japan in the Cold War era—are fading.

Second, Japan will see a generational change in the political leadership of all the major political parties in the next decade. More international-minded, confident, and self-assertive leaders will appear in the top echelon of the leadership.

At the same time, new political waves in Japan—women, the elderly, consumers, environmentalists, and local governments—will gain increasing momentum. Some will push Japan toward a more active role in foreign policy, as exemplified by strong overtures by some prefectures on the Sea of Japan toward the Pacific Soviet Union and pressures from consumers to open agricultural markets. Other political forces may counter with emphasis on heavily domestic issues involving "protection of life." Japan may have to wait for a new generation of leaders as well as political parties to be able to persuade the people that "protection of life" is increasingly linked with the stability and welfare of the world security and economic system to which their voices and commitments will contribute.

Third, Japan must give highest priority in its agenda to strengthening its political leadership and foreign policy-making capabilities in the coming decade. The national debate appears to be starting. It will, without fail, encompass the broad range of issues—political and electoral reform, educational reform, and bureaucratic reform.

Hopefully, painful lessons from the experience in the Gulf will stimulate public interest in and demand for reforming the political system in order to realize and sustain Japan's international new role. After all, a world power is a power with commitment to others. Japan's path to power—global civilian power—must start from the commitment of the public to reform within. In the final analysis, this increasingly seems destined to be the will of the public.

Notes

1. See Charles Krauthammer, "The Unipolar Moment," *Foreign Affairs* 70, no. 1 (1990–91): 24.
2. Jun'ichi Kyogoku, *Gendai minshusei to seijigaku* (Tokyo: Iwanami Shoten, 1969), 170.
3. Robert A. Scalapino, "Perspectives on Modern Japanese Foreign Policy," Robert A. Scalapino, ed., *The Foreign Policy of Modern Japan* (Berkeley and Los Angeles: University of California Press, 1977), 399.
4. On the concept of civilian power: see Hanns W. Maull, "Germany and Japan," *Foreign Affairs* 69, no. 5 (1990–91): 92.

1. Japan's Security Policy in the 1990s

Akihiko Tanaka

The end of the Cold War forces many nations to reformulate or at least rearticulate their respective security policies. Japan is no exception. Japan's defense policy has long assumed that the main threat to its security comes from the North. But with the complete collapse of the Soviet Union, new defense planning in a narrow sense as well as redefinition of a more broad security policy are required for Japan. It is obvious that the end of the Cold War hardly means the beginning of a harmonious and peaceful world. New threats are emerging; Iraq's invasion of Kuwait was the most vivid case in point. Even in East Asia, where on the surface there are no overt military conflicts, international politics is beginning to see some sources of instability: the nuclear threat of North Korea is not yet gone; possible reunification of the Korean Peninsula may entail military aspects; tensions over the Taiwan strait could be heightened; the South China Sea might become a stage of arms competition among the regional states; security implications of the current economic regionalization of China, especially in the post–Deng Xiaoping era, are not clear; and the future of the Russian Federation contains many elements of uncertainty. Japan, a geographical neighbor of Russia, a close ally of the United States, and an advanced industrialized democracy heavily dependent on free flows of international trade, has to reanalyze these current trends in this security environment and reconceptualize its security policy for the coming decades.

In an attempt at such reconceptualization, I will begin by summarizing the basic orientation of Japan's security policy in the postwar period. Thereafter I will analyze the nature of international security in the post–Cold War period; present a new agenda for Japan's security policy in the 1990s; and, finally, discuss some specific policy issues, their feasibility, and domestic constraints that may stand in the way of realizing such new policies.

Basics of Japan's Postwar Security Policy

The basic framework of Japan's security policy is largely determined by the Constitution of 1947 and the security treaty with the United States concluded in 1952 and extensively revised in 1960. One of the reasons why Japan's security policy has sometimes appeared opaque and defense-related debates have often sounded theological is that the historical developments in the postwar period were not anticipated by the Constitution of 1947.

One of the clear characteristics of the Constitution of 1947, written under the strong influence of the U.S. Occupation Forces, was its idealistic and pacific nature. Article 9 stipulates,

Aspiring sincerely to an international peace based on justice and order, the Japanese people forever renounce war as a sovereign right of the nation and the threat or use of force as means of settling international disputes.

In order to accomplish the aim of the preceding paragraph, land, sea, and air forces, as well as other war potential, will never be maintained. The right of belligerence of the state will not be recognized.[1]

Under this constitution, Japan did not possess military forces during most of the occupation period. But with the beginning of the Cold War, the U.S. posture toward Japan's armaments changed, and under Washington's strong pressure, Japan began to equip itself with armed forces under various names: the Police Reserve Forces were created in August 1950 under the direction of General Headquarters (GHQ); the Maritime Security Forces were established in April 1952; the Police Reserve Forces and the Maritime Security Forces were reorganized under the heading of the Hoancho (Security Agency) in August 1952; and in 1954, these forces were further reorganized as the Self-Defense Forces (Jieitai).[2]

The Japanese Self-Defense Forces (SDF) are currently composed of the Ground Self-Defense Force, with 156,000 personnel; the Maritime Self-Defense Force, with fourteen submarines, fifty-five destroyers and frigates (*goeikan*), and seventy-nine reconnaissance airplanes (including fifty P-3Cs); and the Air Self-Defense Force, with nine squadrons of fighters (including 120 F-15J/DJs).[3] In terms of expenditures, Japan's SDF is one of the largest military forces in the world.[4]

Though some in Japan argue that the current Self-Defense Forces constitute "forces" the constitution bans and are therefore unconstitutional, the government of Japan has long maintained that the sovereign right of self-defense is not denied by the constitution and that Japan can maintain such forces as long as they are strictly for the purpose of self-defense. But because of the clear pacific intentions of the constitution, Japan's SDF is restricted in its tasks, area of operation, and the weapons it is allowed to procure. In fact, according to the interpretation of the government of Japan, Japan could constitutionally use "minimally necessary forces" only against "urgent and unjust infringements" when no other means to remove them are available. These three phrases—"urgent and unjust infringement," "no other means available," and "minimally necessary forces"—are usually referred to as the three conditions of resorting to the right of individual self-defense. Beyond such individual self-defense, according to the government interpretation, the constitution does not allow Japan to exercise "collective self-defense."

The tasks of the SDF, stipulated by the 1954 Self-Defense Forces Law, are primarily to defend Japan from direct and indirect aggression and secondarily to preserve public order in Japan, which includes disaster relief activities. The geographic area of operation of the SDF is not clearly specified by law, but the government of Japan declared on various occasions, including a number of Diet sessions, that the SDF's area of operation is not necessarily restricted to Japan's territory, territorial waters, or territorial space but that Japan could not send armed troops to other countries' territory, territorial waters, and territorial space for military purposes because such dispatch goes beyond strict "self-defense" and hence constitutes the exercise of "collective self-defense." On the high seas, there are no legal restrictions against the military operations of the SDF other than the "three conditions of resorting to the right of self-defense." As for the dispatch of the SDF to foreign countries for noncombat purposes, such as in the case of U.N. peacekeeping operations, the government does not interpret such dispatch to be unconstitutional, but until the passage of the International Peace Cooperation Law in June 1992, since the 1954 SDF Law did not list such activity as the SDF's task, it had been considered not within the mandate of the SDF.

The weapons that the SDF can procure are only those "minimally necessary" for self-defense, according to the official interpretation of the constitution. What constitutes "minimally necessary" in each specific circumstance depends on the international situation, the level of military technology, and other conditions, but, in the government's interpretation, such weapons to be used exclusively for destruction of other countries (e.g., ICBMs, long-range bombers, etc.) are under no circumstances to be possessed by Japan. As for nuclear weapons, the government interpretation of the constitution says that the constitution does not prohibit nuclear weapons per se; if nuclear weapons are considered "minimally necessary" for self-defense, the constitution allows Japan to possess them, in the government's interpretation. But the Basic Law of Atomic Energy does not allow Japan to conduct research, develop, or use atomic energy other than for peaceful purposes, and as a signatory of the Nuclear Nonproliferation Treaty, Japan is also prohibited from possessing nuclear weapons. Further, the government declared on various occasions that as a matter of national policy Japan maintains the three nonnuclear principles of not possessing nuclear weapons, not producing them, and not permitting their introduction into Japan.

In addition to the types of weapons, the amount of defense expenditure has also been restricted, though this quantitative restriction is not clearly anchored to any specific law. The most clear restriction was the 1976 cabinet decision to consider 1 percent of the GNP to be the ceiling of the annual defense budget. This 1 percent ceiling was abolished in 1986 and was replaced by a looser and more flexible scheme of deciding the annual budget "within the definite limit" of the Mid-Term Defense Program.

Another area of important self-restraint is that of military exports. In 1967, then Prime Minister Eisaku Sato declared the "Three Principles on Arms Export," which disallowed exports to (1) Communist bloc countries, (2) countries subject to embargoes on arms export under the U.N. Security Council's resolutions, and (3) countries engaged or likely to be engaged in an international conflict. In 1976, Prime Minister

Takeo Miki further tightened the restrictions: (1) arms exports to areas specified in the Three Principles shall not be allowed; (2) arms exports to other areas shall be avoided; and (3) export of arms production–related equipment shall be dealt with in the same way as "arms" are.[5]

In addition to the constitution, the security treaty with the United States provides another important framework for Japan's security policy. The 1960 treaty, formally known as the Treaty of Mutual Cooperation and Security between Japan and the United States of America, is often characterized as being asymmetrical; the United States is obligated by this treaty to defend Japan while Japan is not obligated to defend the United States; the United States is granted the right to maintain its bases in Japan for "the purpose of contributing to the security of Japan and the maintenance of international peace and stability in the Far East," while Japan is not granted similar rights.[6] The former asymmetry has clearly resulted from Japan's constitutional limitations as described above; the Japanese government has maintained that the constitution does not allow Japan to exercise the right of collective self-defense.

Unlike the NATO alliance, the U.S.–Japan alliance, thus created by the security treaty, had not created substantive joint works to improve the effectiveness of the alliance until the mid-1970s. For one thing, quite a few Japanese were inclined against further military cooperation with the United States, especially during the Vietnam War, while many other Japanese took the American presence in the Asian-Pacific region for granted; for another, the Soviet Union had not acquired military capability in the Far East to pose direct threats to Japan until the late 1970s.

But with the Soviet Union military buildup in Asia in the late 1970s, several developments have been made to substantiate the alliance. In 1978, Guidelines for Japan–U.S. Defense Cooperation were agreed upon by the two countries, and on the basis of these guidelines various studies have been conducted; the studies that have been given priority include joint operations, defense of sea lanes of communications, and enhancement of interoperability. In 1981, Prime Minister Zenko Suzuki expressed Japan's willingness to make efforts to protect sea lanes. Joint exercises between the SDF and U.S. forces have increased in number and in scope since the beginning of the 1980s (see table 1.1). As discussed above, exports of military weapons as well as military technology from Japan are strictly controlled. But in 1983, the Japanese government decided not to apply these rules to the United States. Another important

Table 1.1 Japan-U.S. Joint Exercises

Year	GSDF	MSDF	ASDF	UNIFIED
1975		1		
1976		2		
1977		3		
1978		3	3	
1979		3*	11	
1980		3	10	
1981	3	5	12	
1982	4	4*	10	
1983	3	5	12	
1984	5	8*	10	
1985	7	7	13	1
1986	7	7*	12	1
1987	7	7	16	1
1988	7	9*	13	2

* includes the Rim of the Pacific Exercises (RIMPAC)

development is the host-nation support for U.S. forces in Japan; the budget for the host-nation support increased from 163 billion yen in 1981 to 262.4 billion yen in 1989.[7]

To integrate the frameworks created by the Constitution of 1947 and the security treaty with the United States, two guiding concepts were developed in the mid-1970s to early 1980s: the standard defense force *(kibanteki boeiryoku)* and comprehensive security *(sogo anzenhosho)*. According to the National Defense Program Outline adopted on October 29, 1976, the document that embodies the concept of a standard defense force, Japan's defense goal is "the maintenance of a full surveillance posture in peacetime and the ability to cope effectively with situations up to the point of limited and small-scale aggression," and the defense capability of Japan should be "standardized so that, when serious changes in situations so demand, the defense structure can be smoothly adapted to meet such changes." With this sort of defense capability, Japan is supposed to "repel limited and small-scale aggression, in principle, without external assistance. In cases where the unassisted repelling of aggression is not feasible, . . . Japan will continue an unyielding resistance by mobilizing all available forces until such time as cooperation from the United States is introduced, thus rebuffing such aggression." What concretely has materialized under this concept in the

1980s includes the buildup of land defense capability in Hokkaido and of antisubmarine warfare capability around Japan and along the sea lanes one thousand miles south and southwest of Tokyo.

If the goal of the "standard defense force" is to deal with purely military threats by defensive and restrained defense capability with dependence on the United States, the goal of "comprehensive security," developed in the late 1970s to early 1980s, is to define the concept of security more broadly by giving emphasis to nonmilitary aspects of security. The report of a blue-ribbon commission appointed by Prime Minister Masayoshi Ohira defined security in 1980 as "protecting the people's life from various forms of threat" and argued that there should be three levels of efforts for security: "efforts to turn the overall international environment into a favorable one; self-reliant efforts to cope with threats; and as intermediary efforts, efforts to create a favorable international environment within a limited scope while protecting security in solidarity with countries sharing the same ideals and interests."[8]

In retrospect, a number of new developments in Japan's security policy in the 1980s may be interpreted in terms of these three levels as introduced by the report on comprehensive national security. Continuous annual increase in defense expenditures, procurement of highly sophisticated military equipment, and efforts to maintain petroleum reserves (as of 1990, 142 day reserves) are all efforts on the unilateral, self-reliant level. Increasing substantiation of the U.S.–Japan alliance through joint exercises and host-nation support is on the level of cooperation with a like-minded nation. Prime Minister Noboru Takeshita's declaration at the United Nations in 1988 of the three pillars of international cooperation—cooperation for peace, increase of Official Development Assistance, and promotion of international cultural exchange—is a declaration of the intention to promote efforts on the level of preserving peace and stability in the international system.

Thus, by the end of the 1980s, Japan seemed to have reached a point where the Japanese were more or less comfortable with their country's security framework as based on the constitution, the alliance with the United States, and the concepts of standard defense forces and of comprehensive national security. In 1989, 67 percent of the Japanese were in support of the current formula of security policy: a combination of the SDF and the U.S. alliance. Though many criticisms existed as to the organization of the SDF, lack of SDF sustainability, weakness of logistics, and lack of philosophy and coordination in Japan's economic assistance policy, any suggestion of a radical departure from the current framework was not taken seriously. However, radical changes in East-West relations in 1989 and subsequent international events have demanded that the Japanese seriously reexamine their security policy.

Nature of International Security in the 1990s

The end of the Cold War has greatly decreased the probability of the worst possible catastrophe: an all-out nuclear war and a massive conventional attack by the Warsaw Pact army on Western Europe. It is sometimes pointed out that the Cold War has not quite ended in Asia. It is true that in Asia there remain a number of sources of international conflict that were more or less created under the influence of the Cold War. But to the extent that the Cold War means an ideological battle as well as the danger of a nuclear war between the United States and the Soviet Union, it is over even in Asia.

As Saddam Hussein's invasion of Kuwait in August 1990 dramatically showed, however, the end of the Cold War does not entail the end of security issues. Even if it is unlikely that major powers, including the United States and Russia, will engage in large-scale military conflicts with each other, a host of dangers still exist: emergence of adventurer regimes in some countries; proliferation of sophisticated weapons; ethnic conflicts; destabilization of thus-far stable countries; transnational terrorism; supply shortage of critical resources; collapse of the world economy; global environmental destruction; and others. These dangers are related, and more can be added to this list. But many of them are threats not clearly defined and analyzed in traditional analysis of security policy; some of them are not even mentioned. Therefore, now that the time when almost all international conflicts have been interpreted in terms of the East-West confrontation is behind us, systematic efforts to analyze various types of threats are called for in order to place them in proper perspective. The following is an attempt to classify these and other possible threats into four broad groups according to the degree of specificity and identity of actors involved and the degree of the actors' aggressive intentions (figure 1.1).[9]

First, there are threats coming from specific and clearly identifiable

Figure 1.1 Types of International Threats

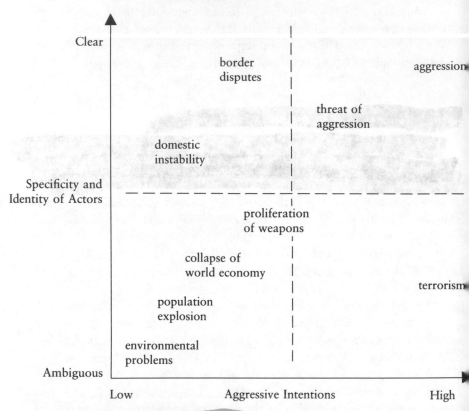

actors with clear aggressive intentions. Adventurous regimes trying to invade or intimidate their neighbors are such threats. Saddam Hussein's Iraq and North Korea, which planned and actually bombed a KAL airliner, are examples par excellence. Security policy in the traditional sense has mainly dealt with this type of threat. Defense planning is often made on the assumption that a certain country could potentially become such an aggressor. In many circumstances, however, it can be difficult to identify the real adventurist until aggression actually takes place.

Second, there are threats to international security in which actors are clearly identifiable but their aggressive intentions are not. Territorial disputes and ethnic conflicts are examples. In territorial disputes, it is not difficult to pinpoint the irredentists. Irredentists' intentions are clear to the extent that they seek to restore the territory they claim. But whether they are willing to resort to arms is not generally clear. In ethnic conflicts, it is not difficult to identify ethnic groups involved in a conflict, but it is not generally clear whether they are willing to resolve the conflict by military means; nor is it always easy to pinpoint the identity and whereabouts of the leadership of a group. Domestic instability is a more elusive threat to international security. Though it is not so difficult to identify which country is politically, economically, and socially unstable, it is not always easy to identify who the significant actors are unless and until a civil war breaks out.

An adventurous regime may emerge as one party in a territorial dispute, the champion of an ethnic group, or a local contender in a civil war. But once the adventurous nature of one party in a conflict is discerned, it should be regarded as the first category of threat. In many other circumstances, however, territorial disputes, ethnic conflicts, and internal instability become militarized not by the existence of an aggressor but as a result of spirals of hostilities and mutual distrust. In these circumstances, it is extremely difficult to identify the aggressors; it may not be morally right to do so.

Third, there are threats in which the identity and whereabouts of actors are not clear but there are clear aggressive intentions. Transnational terrorism is a case in point. Certainly the degree of identifiability may vary. Sometimes such identities as the German Red Army Faction (RAF), the Provisional Irish Republican Army (IRA), or the Japanese Red Army are clear. But not always. And even in such cases of clear identity, it is difficult to pinpoint where the instigators actually are. In some cases, terrorism is supported by governments. For example, Libya and Syria are reported to have training camps for terrorists. Many other countries may be involved in supporting terrorist groups. But the difficulty is that those countries that support terrorists tend to support them within the context of deniability.[10]

The fourth category of threat to international security are those with little clarity of actor identity and lack of aggressive intentions: collapse of the world economy, population explosion, sudden supply shortages of food or critical resources, large-scale natural disasters, and destruction of the global environment. Few countries would intentionally attempt to destroy the world economy or the global environment. Many developing countries are, in fact, trying to control their population growth. Nonetheless, such malfunctions on a global scale are possible and could threaten everyone's security.

Threats that may border on the second and fourth category are those that arise from proliferation of sophisticated and destructive weapons—nuclear, biological, and chemical weapons, and ballistic missiles. Though arms exporters may not intend to destabilize the world, they may be identified: the United States, the U.S.S.R., the People's Republic of China, France, North Korea, Brazil, and others. Sudden supply shortages of food and other resources is another kind of threat that may be difficult to classify. The threat may be caused by an act of an aggressor state or may result from regional conflicts, as in the cases of the first and second oil crises. But the threat may take place because of natural disasters or large-scale accidents (e.g., large-scale nuclear contamination as a result of an accident at a nuclear plant). Given the nature of the distribution system of food and other resources, supply shortage should be considered a phenomenon in the fourth category of threats because, even if the shortage is triggered by an aggressor's decision or by spillover from a regional conflict, the process that could create a sudden supply shortage involves decisions of large numbers of not easily identifiable actors—producer countries, consumer countries, distributing companies, consumers, etc.

Security is a complex problem, and the threats mentioned above are naturally interrelated. Collapse of the world economy or changes in the world economy may aggravate the domestic conditions of a certain country, and in turn lead the country to civil war. Out of such a civil war, an adventurous regime may emerge and, under the pretext of territorial dispute, it may invade a neighboring country. These developments may bring about an acute shortage of natural resources or produce a huge number of refugees. Threats to international security, therefore, do not exist in isolation; they should be grasped comprehensively. But for analytic purposes, it is useful to distinguish different approaches to different types of threat.

For the first category of threat—threat from an adventurer country—deterrence and containment are the primary features of a preventive approach. It is necessary for the adventurer country to be fully aware that aggression does not pay, and it is necessary for outside countries to control the export of arms, military-related technology, and, if necessary, other goods. But deterrence and containment are often most effective after the aggressive nature of the adversary is apparent. If these methods are applied unskillfully when there is still a chance for a civilized regime, they may unintentionally create an adventurous one.

The ultimate preventive approach to this type of threat is to prevent the emergence of an adventurous regime. But there are no easy answers for this. If the Kantian view of international peace—that a republican country does not become adventurous—is correct,[11] assistance to democratic forces in developing countries is one preventive measure. And if economic prosperity is a precondition for democracy in developing countries, economic assistance is another measure. But the difficulties are that economic assistance does not necessarily bring about economic growth and that economic growth does not necessarily create democracy. Economic development under certain circumstances can create instability. Thus, wise judgment is imperative. But, in any case, to reduce the chances of militarization and to limit the scale of military activities, regulation of arms exports to these countries is helpful.

What a country should do after deterrence fails is actually what the traditional defense policy is all about. Each country sometimes tries to defend itself unilaterally and sometimes calls on other countries to help defend it. Alliances may be formed beforehand to make it easier to resort to collective defense. In the post–Cold War era, unilateral defense as well as alliance remain the major means of defense against this type of threat. But as the Gulf War clearly indicated, collective measures carried out under the auspices of the United Nations are also available. To the extent that emergence of an aggressor regime may take place virtually anywhere in the world, however, defensive capacity should include highly mobile forces and technologically sophisticated forces. How these highly mobile forces are organized could be an important issue in the future. Under the current international situation, realistically speaking, if collective measures are to be used, the international community continues to depend on the involvement of the United States, the only country now in possession of such mobile and sophisticated forces.

Among the second category of threats—territorial disputes and ethnic conflicts—measures to prevent militarization include good offices, mediation, arbitration by neighboring countries, regional international organizations or universal international organizations, confidence and security building measures, and arms control. For ethnic conflicts and internal instability, measures designed to facilitate economic development may help. And when those threats exist in undemocratic countries, encouragement of more democratization may also help. (But in some cases, as discussed above, economic development and introduction of some democratic institutions could provide a short-term destabilizing impact.)

After militarization of territorial disputes, ethnic conflicts, and civil disorders, defensive measures that the international community has taken have involved peacekeeping forces of the United Nations or other regional organizations, export control of weapons to the region, and coordination of mechanisms to take care of refugees.

Preventive measures for the third category of threat—transnational terrorism—may include effective police activities in each country, including effective immigration control; effective sharing of information among countries; efforts to persuade as many countries as possible not to support terrorists; and, probably most important, efforts to resolve many ethnic conflicts throughout the world. Beyond preventive measures, few mechanisms exist to effectively defend international security from this type of menace.

The fourth category of threat is most effectively prevented by international cooperation. In preventing further proliferation of sophisticated weapons, arms-exporting countries carry a heavy responsibility. More effective international regimes are called for. To prevent the collapse of the world economy, the roles of the advanced industrial democracies are important; such mechanisms as G-7 summits should become more effective. Sudden supply shortages of food and other resources can be prevented, first, by preventing the first and second categories of threat and, second, by diversifying production sites and technological improvements. For protection of the global environment and prevention of an adverse impact from the population explosion, truly global cooperation is essential. Countries in the North may need to accept a large-scale transfer of wealth to countries in the South in order to reach an effective agreement on certain measures such as protection of tropical forests.

Coping with this type of danger when it actually materializes poses serious difficulties. Certainly there are some unilateral defense measures for some of them. National reserves of food and resources can help in dealing with supply shortages. In many other cases, however, unilateral defense measures can be counterproductive if applied by every country, and often defense measures simply do not exist. Autarky, or a high degree of self-protection, may enable one country to cope with a collapse of the world economy. But if every country takes this posture, the world economy may collapse unnecessarily. While acquiring nuclear or

Figure 1.2 Salient Measures for Threats

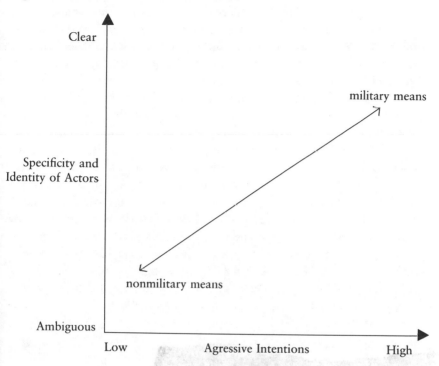

chemical weaponry may be one way for individual nations to deal with the danger arising from proliferation of such weapons, this clearly contributes to the danger everybody was trying to avoid in the first place. Finally, if global environmental problems—global warming, destruction of the ozone layer, pollution of the oceans—become really serious, there are no effective defense measures. In other words, for this type of threat, prevention is far more important than defense, and prevention requires wide-scale cooperation.

Examining the four categories of threat, we see that preventive and defensive measures involve different mechanisms. But generally speaking, threats located near the upper-right corner of figure 1.1 seem to require more military means, and threats near the lower-left corner call for nonmilitary means (see figure 1.2). Furthermore, most of these measures are more effective if they are applied collectively rather then unilaterally. To cope with an adventurer regime, the solidarity of the opposing countries is essential. To prevent terrorist activities, information-sharing among countries is necessary. For the international community to prevent territorial disputes, ethnic conflicts, and civil disorders from spilling over, coordinated action by neighboring countries is useful. And it is almost impossible to achieve protection of the global environment without international cooperation.

To say that international cooperation is necessary, however, does not mean that it is easy. On the contrary, to the extent that the "hegemonic stability" theory has some validity, international cooperation among major countries when there are no dominant powers is difficult.[12] If, due to the relative decline of U.S. economic power, the United States takes either an isolationist policy or an extreme unilateral policy, it may be difficult to forge a consensus to create a cooperative scheme in dealing with the above security threats in the 1990s. But there are grounds for cautious optimism; with the end of acute ideological conflicts between the West and the East, it has finally become possible to utilize the framework of the U.N. Security Council to cope with security issues. Multinational efforts to condemn and contain Iraq may be the beginning of real international security cooperation in the 1990s.

The Security Policy of Japan in the 1990s

If the nature of international security in the 1990s is as I have described above, then what should Japan do? What are the deficiencies in Japan's security policy and policy-making apparatus? What are the necessary changes? What are the constraints on making changes?

First, the basic elements of Japan's defense posture in the postwar era do not need to be altered; limited capability with a self-defense doctrine plus reliance on the security treaty with the United States are still valid in the 1990s. It is true that the main source of concern against which the Japanese defense apparatus and the U.S. alliance had been created—the Soviet threat—has virtually disappeared. But this change, though important, does not immediately justify a wholesale change in the basic elements of Japanese security policy, including its alliance with the United States. The concept of a "standard defense force" and the principle of "defensive defense" are still—in fact, more—valid after the disappearance of the Soviet threat. Furthermore, the Japan–U.S. alliance has other important functions besides coping with the Soviet threat.

First, besides the threat from the Soviet Union, other potential threats have always existed in East Asia. North Korea may pose the first type of threat once it acquires nuclear weapons. If the current North Korean regime collapses because of internal difficulties, the Korean Peninsula can be destabilized. China, currently no military threat to Japan, is modernizing its military, most notably its navy, and in the long term can become a potential source of military concern in the region. Therefore, the U.S.–Japan alliance is still serving the function of preventing such potential threats in the region.

Second, the alliance shows the joint commitment of the two largest economic powers in the world to liberal democratic values and to their close economic cooperation. The preamble of the security treaty says that the two countries desire "to uphold the principles of democracy, individual liberty, and the rule of law," and "to encourage closer economic cooperation between them."[13]

Third, the Japan–U.S. alliance has served as one of the most important premises of international security relations in East Asia; as the preamble and article 6 of the treaty indicate, the security treaty stipulates continuing U.S. engagement in the Far East in addition to U.S. commitment to defend Japan. The fear that an independent Japan without the U.S. alliance would actually become militaristic, irresponsible, or less trustworthy is exaggerated, and I believe the current democratic political system can prevent Japan from becoming so. But it is a fact that there are such widespread fears among neighboring countries—fears totally understandable given Japanese aggression in the area half a century ago and the current overwhelming Japanese economic influence in the region. And to the extent that psychological factors actually affect substance in international politics, the Japan–U.S. alliance continues to serve the important role of reassuring Asian nations that Japan will not become a militaristic power again.

In other words, the basic orientation of efforts on the two levels of comprehensive national security—the level of its defense efforts and the level of cooperation with like-minded countries, especially the United States—need not be changed.

An unchanged basic orientation, however, does not necessarily mean that defense policy does not have to be reviewed. Indeed, the end of the Cold War forces Japan to apply major revisions to the current defense policy in the following two respects. First, the composition of defense capability must be reviewed. During the so-called New Cold War era in the 1980s, the Self-Defense Forces' organization and arms procurement, though they were well within the boundary of the concept of "standard defense force," were geared toward defense against the threat from the North, emphasizing antisubmarine capabilities in cooperation with U.S. forces. And that was not a mistake at all.

Now that Russia can hardly pose an actual military threat, however, this emphasis on the threat from the North and on antisubmarine capabilities should be reviewed, taking into consideration the future development of the U.S.–Russian disarmament in the northwestern Pacific region.

As for the Ground SDF, the new Mid-Term Defense Plan (1991–95) sets its personnel ceiling at 153,000 whereas its actual capacity is 180,000. But one may wonder whether it is still appropriate to station two mixed forces of twelve divisions in each base nationwide. It might be more appropriate for the post–Cold War standard defense force to trim off personnel and maintain a few mobile forces instead.

As for the Maritime SDF, what will be the mission of destroyers, frigates, and submarines? Will Japan still need destroyers and frigates equipped with the very sophisticated anti-air aegis system? What are the reasons for continued procurement of antisubmarine PC-3s?

While it is natural for the Air SDF to try to cover the entire territory, is it not appropriate to reconsider the continued procurement of such an expensive fighter as the F-15 and the development of the FSX? On the other hand, we should be prepared for a new threat from ballistic missiles intentionally or accidentally launched or stray missiles from nearby regional conflicts. North Korea's missiles possibly with nuclear warheads are the cases in point. These possibilities require that Japan seriously consider the desirability of creating an effective antimissile defense system.

In any event, the SDFs need to be trimmed, particularly in light of the imminent decrease in the proportion of the younger generation in the overall national population in the near future. The SDF reserve system should thus be significantly reformed and its division structure reorganized. The future plan should include a policy to significantly reduce SDF personnel while at the same time increasing the number but lowering the average age of the current 47,900 SDF reserves.

Furthermore, it is about time to integrate the three SDFs into a more unified structure. In order to fulfill the mission of self-defense of such an island nation as Japan, as has been long suggested, three separate military structures of land, air, and maritime forces are inefficient, especially given the decrease of population; a more unified structure is called for.

Secondly, together with these revisions of SDF personnel, physical defense capability should be reduced for the time being, or at least frozen. It is true that a large portion (78.8 percent in FY 1991) of Japan's defense expenditure has been occupied by obligatory expenses determined at the beginning of the budget planning, such as personnel expenses, food and other overhead expenses, and payment for the procurements already ordered. It is equally true that in the new Mid-Term Defense Plan, expenses for frontal equipment, including arms, are to be reduced by 2.3 percent annually. Nevertheless, total defense expenditure must be reduced or frozen. When the defense capability composition is readjusted to the new situation and environment, it should be possible, first of all, to reduce personnel expenses as well as expenses for frontal equipment. Secondly, under certain circumstances (when, for instance, a certain degree of naval disarmament is advanced in the western Pacific), the Defense Agency can cancel the procurement of equipment that had already been ordered, if it can induce high-level political decisions. Thirdly, it will be very important to reduce defense expenditures if Japan wishes to play a constructive role in international politics, particularly in Asia. While it is true that the defense expenditures of Japan's neighboring countries have been on the rise, they do not immediately pose any direct threat to Japan. Moreover, if Japan does not reduce its defense expenditure despite the end of the Cold War, this can be possibly interpreted as a symbol of Japan's remilitarization intention, regardless of the true content of the expenditure. In order to symbolically demonstrate to the world that Japan does not have any ulterior motive behind such activities as participation in the U.N.'s peacekeeping operations and the SDF's contribution to international relief activities, Japan must reduce its defense expenditure.

What is clearly deficient in Japan's effort in the post–Cold War period, however, are its efforts on the third level—to preserve and enhance the peace and stability of the international system. It is true that then Prime Minister Noboru Takeshita declared three pillars of international cooperation in 1988. But the inadequacy of Japan's policy-making apparatus—including the legal system—was clearly revealed by the reaction—or lack of reaction, which may more properly be called paralysis—of the Japanese government to Iraq's aggression against Kuwait. The following are possible changes that Japan should make in its policies to cope with each of the four categories of threat to international society.

Japan has no unilateral military means for coping with the first category of threat—emergence of an adventurer state—unless such a threat is directed against Japan. If a clearly adventurer regime appears, as in the case of Iraq, Japan should support the military efforts of the United States and other countries in order to deter aggression and should join in the efforts to contain the aggressor regime. If, eventually, a U.N. force is created to cope with this type of threat and Japan's neighbors agree, Japan should send the SDF to join the U.N. forces, though this may entail constitutional debates in Japan, which I will describe below. But in the meantime, because there are no effective U.N. forces with highly mobile and sophisticated weapons, Japan should give financial, logistical, and other nonmilitary support to multinational forces created on an ad hoc basis.

The best way to prevent an adventurer regime from launching an invasion is to prevent the emergence of such a regime. For that purpose, establishment of a stable democratic regime and economic development are the best measures. Though this method is not a panacea, Japan could still offer economic assistance to developing countries so that democratic values and economic development are promoted; for example, improvement of the infrastructure of communication networks and promotion of primary and secondary education can, at least in the long term, contribute to both democratic values and economic development.

To deal with the second category of threat—territorial disputes, ethnic conflicts, and internal instability—Japan should play a facilitating role when appropriate and encourage peaceful resolution by, if necessary, extending inducements in terms of economic assistance to the parties concerned. Japan could extend support to multilateral peacekeeping efforts in terms of financial and human resources. The International Peace Cooperation Law, passed by the Diet in June 1992 after more than a year-long debate, finally established a legal framework within which the SDF could participate in the U.N. peacekeeping operations. But the current law still limits Japanese participation to mostly logistical support for peacekeeping operations. It should be revised to enable full-scope participation in U.N. peacekeeping operations.

The third category of threat—transnational terrorism—seems most effectively tackled by effective policy operations in each country as well as by the sharing of information. Japan should increase cooperation with other countries in developing highly sophisticated bomb-detection equipment. It should also make efforts to prevent thefts of nuclear materials by terrorists.

Measures to cope with the fourth category of threat—global problems—really require international cooperation. If Japan is preoccupied with narrow and short-term national interests, let alone small sectorial interests within Japan, multilateral efforts will not succeed. In order to make the Uruguay Round successful, Japan should agree to stop the banning of rice imports, for example. On the issue of proliferation of sophisticated and destructive weapons, Japan should consider using positive inducements in terms of economic assistance to those countries that comply with nonproliferation. To cope with global environmental problems and various forms of pollution, Japan should extend its financial as well as technological support.

To achieve the above changes, Japan has to overcome various domestic constraints—legal systems, current bureaucratic frameworks, domestic politics, and public opinion. Let us examine such obstacles to (1) more active participation in international peacekeeping and security-enhancing activities, (2) more flexible and effective use of economic assistance for security purposes as defined here, and (3) a more effective central decision-making apparatus under the prime minister that can act promptly and properly in an international crisis.

First, regarding the issue of more active participation in international peacekeeping and security-enhancing activities, the strength of constraints vary according to the use of the SDF. If the SDF is to be dispatched for unilateral military action, the constitution should be revised. And revision of the constitution is extremely difficult because it requires the support of a two-thirds majority of the members of each House as well as majority support in a national referendum. Under current circumstances, it is particularly impossible to change the constitution because opposition parties and a sizeable number of LDP members would oppose a revision that would allow the dispatch of the SDF for unilateral military action. Even if the LDP were united, since it does not have a two-thirds majority in the House of Representatives (nor does it have even a simple majority in the House of Councillors), it could not pass such a resolution in the Diet.[14] In any case, if Japan were to revise the constitution to allow for *unilateral* military action abroad, that would create waves of international concern and would destabilize international politics in Asia. Therefore, this is not a desirable course.

As for a possible dispatch of SDF personnel to a U.N. force as defined by article 42 of the U.N. charter,[15] its constitutionality is debatable. It seems possible to argue that participation in a U.N. force as defined by article 42 is consistent with the renunciation of war and that military capacity to be used by such a U.N. force has nothing to do with "force" as banned by the constitution.[16] But the official government interpretation of the constitution said in 1980 that if the mission of a "U.N. force" includes "the use of force," the SDF is not constitutionally allowed to participate in it.[17] Thus, to realize such a dispatch, at least a change in the official government interpretation is necessary. But during the Diet session in the autumn of 1990, Prime Minister Kaifu stated that he was not planning to change this interpretation. Further, since the SDF Law does not include such a mission in the SDF's objectives, a change in that law or a special law is necessary.

If the dispatch of the SDF is to a U.N. force whose mission does not include the use of force, the government interpretation of the constitution says that it is constitutional. But in any case, if a U.N. force is made under article 42, a strong case can be made to facilitate dispatch of the SDF even if the mission of the U.N. force includes military operations, though since the U.N. charter allows members to decide their forms of participation, Japan would opt for a noncombat mission for its SDF.

A slightly tricky case is that of a multinational force authorized by the U.N. Security Council, such as a multinational force to enforce economic sanctions against Iraq. To the extent that such multinational forces have a mission involving "use of force," sending the SDF to participate in such forces is unconstitutional in the current government interpretation. But if the "use of force" is not included in the mission, Japan could send the SDF pending changes of the SDF Law or a new special law.

Sending the SDF on other U.N. peacekeeping missions is legally less tricky, because the "use of force" is not generally included in U.N. peacekeeping operations, and this was made possible by the International Peace Cooperation Law mentioned above.

As discussed above, given the nature of threats to international security in the coming decades, the role of nonmilitary means for security is increasing. Because Japan imposes strict limitations on the use of military capacity, as described above in detail, economic assistance should be given more priority than before for the purposes of security policy in a broad sense. But Japan has in many cases refrained from attaching political conditions to its economic assistance because, it is explained, Japan's aid is motivated by humanitarian considerations and the awareness of "interdependence" among nations. Furthermore, Japan's aid is conducted on the "request" principle *(yosei shugi)*, which requires that Japan give economic assistance only when a request is made from a foreign country. It is true that Japan can use its own criteria to select various requests, but passivity is apparent in this formula.

However, a clear departure of policy was made in the spring of 1991, when Prime Minister Toshiki Kaifu announced that "Japan will pay full attention in the implementation of ODA to the following points of the recipient countries: (1) trends in military expenditure; (2) trends in the development, production, etc., of weapons of mass destruction such as atomic weapons and missiles; (3) trends in the export and import of weapons; and (4) efforts for promoting democratization, the introduction of a market-oriented economy, and the security of basic human rights and freedoms."[18] Furthermore, on June 30, 1992, the Japanese government officially concluded an "Official Development Assistance Charter"—the first official document to describe the philosophy and principles of Japan's aid—which reconfirms Kaifu's guidelines.[19] Though implementation of the new guidelines may raise difficulties in concrete areas, it is important to make them known to all recipient nations and to use them as means to persuade such nations to accomplish the goals of the new guidelines.

In addition to these difficulties on the level of policy, there is a more difficult problem in decision-making—the extremely decentralized and overlapping nature of decision-making on economic assistance. Grants are generally controlled by the Ministry of Foreign Affairs, but yen loans are controlled by the Ministry of International Trade and Industry; aid through international organizations is controlled by the Ministry of Foreign Affairs and the Ministry of Finance. Implementation of economic assistance is shared by virtually all ministries of the Japanese government. Even though the four–ministry/agency meeting (MOFA, MITI, MOF, and Economic Planning Agency) is supposed to coordinate

Japan's entire aid policy, it is not clear whether this mechanism is effective for flexible management of economic assistance for security policy. Since Japan's Security Council, created in 1986 to deliberate on important issues of defense and other emergencies, is not explicitly in charge of economic assistance, there are no cabinet-level coordinating meetings or staff.[20]

One of the major characteristics of Japan's bureaucracy are its highly autonomous and independent ministries and agencies. Ministers and parliamentary vice-ministers are appointed by the prime minister mostly from among Diet members. But parliamentary vice-ministers are generally powerless. Aside from these two posts, there are virtually no political appointees; the highest-ranking position after the minister, that of administrative vice-minister, is occupied by the most successful career bureaucrats, whose appointment is generally made by seniority and reputation among fellow bureaucrats. And because of a more than thirty-year-long symbiosis between the ruling LDP and the bureaucracy, in many policy areas, standard operating procedures have been firmly established. Therefore, unless the prime minister is really determined, he cannot introduce new policies, especially if they have something to do with the turfs of multiple ministries and agencies.

In security policy, there have been several attempts to create a cabinet-level coordinating mechanism: in 1956, the Defense Council was established, and in 1986 it was replaced by the Security Council. The Security Council was created because the Defense Council had become a largely ratifying body rather than a deliberative body. But the Security Council, composed of the prime minister, the foreign minister, the finance minister, the chief cabinet secretary, the chairman of the National Public Safety Commission, the director of the Defense Agency, and the director of the Economic Planning Agency, has also ended up being a ratifying body. And with the establishment of the Security Council, a reorganization of the Prime Minister's Office was also made; several new coordinating offices were created: the Councillor's Office on Internal Affairs, the Councillor's Office on External Affairs, the Security Affairs Office, and the Research and Intelligence Office. But during the international crisis triggered by Iraq's invasion of Kuwait, the coordinating mechanism under the prime minister did not appear to work effectively. Japan's economic sanctions and other measures were decided without convening Security Council meetings.

Part of the reason that the central decision-making system lacks effective coordination is because the Prime Minister's Secretariat is understaffed and, furthermore, is staffed by bureaucrats on loan from various ministries. The number of staff of the entire Cabinet Secretariat is 176; within it, the Councillor's Office on External Affairs is staffed by nineteen bureaucrats; the Security Affairs Office, by twenty-four; and the Research and Intelligence Office, by twenty-four.

It is of course the role of the chief cabinet secretary to coordinate the views of various ministries and agencies. But because the chief cabinet secretary is chosen from among the members of the Diet, he or she may not be the right person to coordinate international affairs issues. A prime minister is supported in foreign affairs by his secretaries, one of whom is sent by the foreign minister. But because the position of secretary to a prime minister is not very high in the Foreign Ministry's bureaucratic ladder, he or she may not wield effective power over the Foreign Ministry, let alone over other ministries. Heads of various offices of the Cabinet Secretariat are generally sent by different ministries, also; it is difficult to expect them to play a coordinative role. In other words, a prime minister of Japan has no official international affairs advisors, powerful and independent of each ministry.

Given the nature of parliamentary democracy and the tradition of a strong and talented bureaucracy, it may not be wise to import the U.S. system of the National Security Council and its staff. But it is possible and necessary to strengthen the staff of the offices in the Cabinet Secretariat. Furthermore, prime ministers should create interministerial coordination frameworks in normal times so that they can be utilized at times of crisis.

In sum, because Japan's constitution precludes the use of military force as a means to achieve national goals, its security policy is constrained in comparison with, for example, the United States, but Japan could still contribute to the enhancement of international security in the 1990s at least in the following ways: (1) Japan could participate more actively in U.N. peacekeeping operations; (2) being a country with the self-imposed restraints of not having nuclear weapons and of not exporting weapons, Japan could engage more actively in creating and maintaining international regimes that prevent proliferation of sophisticated weapons; and (3) for the purpose of nonproliferation as well as other purposes—resolution of international conflicts, promotion of democratic values, promotion of environmental protection—Japan could use economic assistance and other financial means as positive inducements.

Conclusion

The end of the Cold War was brought about without a frontal military clash between the West and the East; the Western allies were able to maintain military preparedness without collapsing their economies while the Soviet Union and its allies almost destroyed their economies in the process of building up their military. The sound economic base of the capitalist world seems to have been critical in bringing about the West's "victory" in the Cold War. In fact, it is a rare phenomenon in world history that a change of this magnitude was achieved without a major war, and this fact clearly encourages the direction that Japan has taken since its defeat from a disastrous war. A world in which major international issues are resolved without wars is a good world for a people who "have determined to preserve [their] security and existence, trusting in the justice and faith of the peace-loving peoples of the world."[21] It is, therefore, in the Japanese basic security interest to maintain this trend of nonmilitary conflict resolution.

But clearly, the end of the Cold War does not mean the complete end of the usefulness of force as a means of national policy. Military means have also played important roles in ending the Cold War; strategic nuclear stability as well as conventional military efforts have deterred the actual use of military force in resolving conflicts. Furthermore, as examined above, there can be regimes in the world that may be tempted to use force to achieve their ambitions, toward whom military deterrence is still an essential element. In other words, military means are still necessary to deter those who are ready to use force to achieve their ambitions. If Japan's basic security interest is to preserve a world of nonmilitary conflict resolution, it is essential for Japan to support efforts to contain possible and actual aggressors. If the United States is the only military power in the world that can contain potential aggressions, it is in Japan's security interest to support the United States. If the United Nations is regaining authority and effectiveness in coping with aggressor states, it is in Japan's security interests to cooperate with it.

To prevent other types of threats to international security—regional arms races, ethnic conflicts, instability in many countries, terrorism, a collapse of the world economy, environmental disasters, proliferation of sophisticated weapons—is also in Japan's security interest. Japanese economic activities are global, and thus armed conflicts in distant places can affect Japanese economy directly. Japan should use all the means at its disposal—including ODA—to prevent further proliferation of sophisticated weapons throughout the world. Those global issues, such as the state of the world economy and environmental problems, know no geographical limits. Japan's security interests are now global.

The security situation within Japan's proximity, nevertheless, is still crucial to Japan; peace and stability in Asia and the Pacific is clearly the most important security interest of Japan. The Japan–U.S. alliance, among others, is the basic premise of almost all important international relations in the area, without which the very base of the current economic growth of the Asian-Pacific region seems extremely fragile. Also important are Japan's good relations with other neighbors in the area. Given the Japanese wartime conduct in the area as well as the current increasing economic integration with the countries in the area, Japan should be attentive to the views of its neighbors. Sometimes, Japan's policy to strengthen the solidarity of the Japan–U.S. alliance can invite criticism from these neighbors; Kaifu's U.N. Peace Cooperation Bill was the most recent such instance. I believe that Japan should accept such awkward situations as a price of its past history of militarism. But it is in the security interest of Japan to persuade its neighbors that improvement of Japan–U.S. relations in fact contributes to the peace and stability of the region more than would a deterioration of relations between Tokyo and Washington.

Finally, it is crucial to the security interest of Japan to improve the quality of its decision-making. For a country proud of its global economic activities and restrained from the use of military means, information gathering, the correct analysis of information, and prompt action based on such analysis are essential. The quality of both routine decision-making and crisis decision-making is in need of improvement. Japan's bureaucratic system for handling international affairs has not changed much since the end of World War II, when Japan wanted to become a Switzerland in the Pacific. Some forty years later, in order to become a light-armed, responsible economic global power, Japan now needs expansion as well as reorganization of its system for making decisions about international affairs.

Notes

1. This is from the most commonly used English translation of the Japanese Constitution. However, the Japanese original allows for various interpretations that may not be easy to derive from this English translation. For example, according to one interpretation, the first sentence in the second paragraph should be translated as "Land, sea, and air forces, as well as other war potential, in order to accomplish the aim mentioned in the preceding paragraph [i.e., to settle international disputes], will never be maintained." See Soichi Sasaki, *Nihonkoku Kenpo-ron* (The Japanese Constitution) (Tokyo: Yuhikaku, 1949), 233; Hitoshi Ashida, *Shin-Kempo Kaishaku* (Interpretation of the New Constitution) (Tokyo: Daiyamondosha, 1946), 36.
2. For a concise review of Japan's "rearmament," see Makoto Momoi,"Basic Trends in Japanese Security Policies," in Robert A. Scalapino, ed., *The Foreign Policy of Modern Japan* (Berkeley: University of California Press, 1977), 341–64. For a more detailed documentary, see Yomiuri Shimbun Sengoshi Han, *"Saigunbi" no kiseki* (Tracks of "Rearmament") (Tokyo: Yomiuri Shimbunsha, 1981).
3. Boei-cho, *Heisei Gannen-ban Boei Hakusho* (1989 White Paper of Defense) (Tokyo: Okurasho Insatsukyoku, 1989), 316–17, 325.
4. Japan's 1988 defense expenditure was $15,298 million (at 1985 prices and exchange rates), compared with the United Kingdom's $22,637 million, France's $21,903 million, and West Germany's $20,870 million. See International Institute for Strategic Studies (IISS), *The Military Balance, 1989–1990* (London: IISS, 1989), 208–11.
5. According to the U.S. Arms Control and Disarmaments Agency (ACDA), Japan made "arms exports worth $320 million in 1983, $280 million in 1984, $90 million in 1985, and $20 million in 1986." Since the ACDA's definition of "arms" includes parts of weapons and communications and electronic equipment, Japan's "arms exports" seem to constitute such "dual-use equipment."
6. Article 5 of the Japan–U.S. security treaty stipulates, "Each Party recognizes that an armed attack against either Party in the territories under the administration of Japan would be dangerous to its own peace and safety and declares that it would act to meet the common danger in accordance with its constitutional provisions and processes." Article 6 stipulates the U.S. right to use bases in Japan as follows: "For the purpose of contributing to the security of Japan and the maintenance of international peace and stability in the Far East, the United States of America is granted the use of facilities and areas in Japan by its land, air and naval forces."

7. *Boei Hakusho* (Defense White Paper) (Tokyo: Defense Agency, 1981, 1989).

8. The Comprehensive National Security Study Group, ed., Report on Comprehensive National Security, July 2, 1980, 7. The *1989 Gaiko Seisho* (1989 Diplomatic Blue Paper) (Tokyo: Ministry of Foreign Affairs) virtually gives official endorsement of the three levels as suggested in the report. According to the Blue Paper, the three pillars of Japan's security policy are "(1) active diplomacy to make the international environment as peaceful and stable as possible, (2) smooth and effective operation of the Japan–U.S. security system, and (3) preparation of high-quality defense capability necessary for self-defense." *Heisei Gan-nen ban Gaiko Seisho* (1989 Diplomatic Blue Paper), 15.

9. This section is a revised version of the analysis I made in "International Security and Japan's Contribution in the 1990s," *Japan Review of International Affairs* 4, no. 2 (Fall–Winter 1990): 199–208.

10. Karl W. Deutsch, *The Analysis of International Relations,* 3d ed. (Englewood Cliffs, N.J.: Prentice Hall, 1988), 193–202; *Strategic Survey, 1985–1986* (London: International Institute of Strategic Studies, 1986), 19–28.

11. Immanuel Kant, *Perpetual Peace* (1795), an English translation found, for example, in M. G. Forsyth, H. M. A. Keens-Soper, and P. Savigear, eds., *The Theory of International Relations* (London: Allen and Unwin, 1970), 200–244; Michael W. Doyle, "Liberalism and World Politics," *American Political Science Review* 80, no. 4 (December 1986): 1151–69. According to Doyle, democracies have rarely fought each other for the last two centuries. Skepticism about this view also abounds. See John J. Measheimer, "Back to the Future: Instability in Europe after the Cold War," *International Security* 15, no. 1 (Summer 1990): 5–56.

12. There is voluminous literature on the "hegemonic stability" theory. See, for example, Robert Gilpin, *War and Change in World Politics* (Cambridge: Cambridge University Press, 1981); Robert Keohane, *After Hegemony* (Princeton: Princeton University Press, 1984).

13. Article 2 of the treaty stipulates, "The Parties will contribute toward the further development of peaceful and friendly international relations by strengthening their free institutions, by bringing about a better understanding of the principles upon which these institutions are founded, and by promoting conditions of stability and well-being. They will seek to eliminate conflict in their international economic collaboration policies and will encourage collaboration between them."

14. In the case of the House of Representatives, the LDP government can dissolve it to try to increase the number of LDP members. But under the current electoral district system—the multiple-seat constituency system—it is empirically impossible for the LDP to gain a two-thirds majority. The political reform efforts, currently contemplated within the LDP, include the introduction of a single-constituency district system, which would theoretically make it possible for the LDP to gain a two-thirds majority. But even

then, unless a drastic change in the electoral system for the House of Councillors is made, it is impossible to gain a two-thirds majority in the Upper House.

15. No U.N. forces under article 42 have been created since the five permanent members of the Security Council failed to reach agreements to create such forces as stipulated by article 43 in 1947.
16. A commission established in the LDP headed by Ichiro Ozawa maintains this interpretation.
17. However, it is not clear whether the term "U.N. force" as used in the government interpretation refers to the same "U.N. force" described under article 42 of the U.N. charter.
18. Ministry of Foreign Affairs, *Diplomatic Bluebook 1991* (Tokyo: The Japan Times, 1992), 131.
19. For the text of the new ODA Charter, see Ministry of Foreign Affairs, *Japan's ODA 1992* (Tokyo: Association for Promotion of International Cooperation, 1993), 193–96.
20. It is possible, however, that the prime minister can convene a cabinet meeting with the participation of related ministers and can require, for example, the Councillor's Office on External Affairs, in the Prime Minister's Office, to coordinate ministers. Besides the relative weakness of the Prime Minister's Office as discussed in the text below, ad hoc coordination may result in a lack of coherence without producing flexibility.
21. Preamble of the Japanese Constitution.

2. Technology and the Setting for Japan's Agenda

Taizo Yakushiji

Debates on Japan's international agenda would not have been seriously entertained during the height of the Cold War. Japan's role was trivial, and the international system was largely managed by two superpowers.

If a fresh need for such a debate emerges today, it has two causes. First, the superpowers are less "super"; that is, they have relatively declined. Second, Japan's power has risen. How has it risen? Of course, Japan has become economically and technologically powerful, but the political and military implications of this remain unclear.

Technology increases economic strength and thus is conventionally regarded as playing a role in the rise of nations. Japan is a notable example. However, less familiar is the argument that a position of technological leadership carries the seeds of national decline. The reasons are threefold.

First, diffusion of technologies causes the rise of formidable contenders. Competitors eventually emerge when they have succeeded in technological "emulation," meaning technological "copying" plus a significant "improvement."[1]

Second, technological supremacy promotes a blind belief in economic rationality and efficiency. For example, economically efficient mass production with standardized technology is believed to add wealth, so that new technological endeavors that would shut down the current profitable production lines are rejected. An example is General Electric's rejection of transistors in the 1950s.

Third, when a nation assumes a technological lead, it easily develops strong "techno-parochialism," leading to technological arrogance. This arrogance blinds people to the secret of preeminence, that is, "emulous power." Without the copying and improvement of advanced technologies both abroad and at home, technological leads quickly erode.[2]

The international system is constituted of all sovereign states. Therefore, the decline or rise of major states can disturb the system. Technology, through its impact on national power, plays a critical role in the structure and stability of the international system.

This is why Japan's technological agenda is so significant. If the superpowers had not declined, Japan's technological agenda could remain largely of domestic or commercial interest; that is, Japan would seek to enhance its own technological capabilities or hinder their erosion.

However, as the superpowers are decaying in both economic and technological leadership, and as Japan has risen to technological preeminence, the agenda is no longer just domestic, but truly global in its impact.

America's "Techno-Bashing" of Japan

For the time being, Japan's technological agenda is essentially *bilateral* in relation to the United States. The reasons for this are the subject of this section.

Since the mid-1980s, the United States has increased its "techno-bashing" of Japan. This includes the argument that U.S. firms do not enjoy "symmetrical access" to Japanese firms' research and development (R&D) or the government's research consortia, the IBM suit against Hitachi for alleged industrial spying, the violent U.S. reaction to Toshiba H.I.'s sale of propeller technology to the U.S.S.R., efforts by the United States to restrict technology transfer in the development of the FSX aircraft, blockage of the sale of Fairchild Industries to a Japanese firm, and U.S. efforts to promote high-definition television (HDTV).

1. "Techno-Revisionism"

Recently, an ominous new symptom has emerged. It is "techno-revisionism," which is more serious than the general revisionist thesis about

Japan that has risen in the West. Unlike the "general" revisionists, the techno-revisionists see Japan as a genuine Western capitalist economy, but also as an adversary that exercises frontal attacks against the United States. The battle is one of technological warfare, in which Japan mobilizes the full capacity of its technological strength to invade and then occupy U.S. markets. A typical expression of this view is "Technology and Competitiveness: The New Policy Frontier," by B. R. Inman and D. F. Burton, Jr.[3]

Criticizing past American foreign policy approaches, which were overly based on military considerations and neglected the overriding importance of commercial technologies, the authors insist that national security can no longer be viewed in exclusively military terms; economic security and industrial competitiveness are also vital. They call for a shift of American foreign policy, and contend that, since important political allies are often hard-nosed economic competitors, the U.S. establishment can no longer afford a cavalier attitude toward international competition in industrial technology with allies.

Inman and Burton do not explicitly say that U.S. foreign policy should rethink its diplomatic ties with Japan, but they imply it. In the five cases they examine (consumer electronics, semiconductors, superconductors, the FSX fighter, and high-definition television), they delineate how American inventions and subsequent market dominance were exploited by Japanese superior productive skills. Then they warn U.S. foreign policymakers that today's commercial technologies are all related in a "food chain," in which one technology eats away the next technology, this second technology washes out the third technology, and so on. In the end, one decisive technology controls all related technologies. The implication of the "techno–food chain" thesis is obvious: a division of labor in technology based on international cooperation would jeopardize the technological leadership of the United States.

2. *"Techno-Containment"*

Different in the style of argument from that of "techno-revisionism" but more or less in the same tone is the argument by Charles H. Ferguson's article in the *Harvard Business Review*.[4] His thesis might be regarded as typical of the "techno-containment" theory.

Ferguson assumes that nearly all industrial products are being digitalized and that the American digital information systems industry is threatened by the "predatory behavior" of Japanese *keiretsu* companies. He argues that Japanese *keiretsu*, or affiliate corporate relations, companies block foreign applications for the Japanese patents and deny foreign competitors' access to technologies and markets over which Japanese industries have control. Then, Ferguson suggests that building an appropriate corporate organizational complex will allow U.S. and European companies to secure their supply bases against strategic pressures exerted by the integrated Japanese competitors to obtain sufficient financial returns from the commercialization of their own innovative designs.

Politically important is the fact that Ferguson, too, rejects the principle of a division of labor between the United States and Japan in which Japanese producers would specialize in commodity manufacturing, while U.S. companies would continue to lead by virtue of their command of the higher value-added activities of design, software, systems integration, and marketing. His rationale is very similar to that of Inman and Burton's "technological food chain." Ferguson insists that if this division of labor is adopted, American companies will in effect become the local design and marketing subsidiaries for Japanese competitors, who will exploit most revenue returns.

Under this logic, he says that now is the time to build on the embryonic alliance initiated by IBM and European companies, including companies from Korea, Taiwan, and Singapore—that is, a multinational version of *keiretsu*.

3. "Techno-Containment" in the Late Nineteenth Century

In 1896, two years before the Spanish-American War, Ernest E. Williams, a British writer, wrote a book entitled *Made in Germany*. At that time, the United States, though its industrial economy was growing very rapidly, was still a latecomer. Henry Ford's famous Model-T had not yet come out on the market, and most American auto manufacturers were busy imitating German and French manufacturing technologies. Before Thomas Edison's new light bulbs hit the market and GE was founded in 1892, there were already well-established electrical illumination industries in Europe. The industrial rivalry then was not between the United States and Japan but between England and Germany.

Williams warned,

Seeing how many inventions have England for a birthplace, it is obvious that the present proportions of German industry can only have been attained by a careful imitation of those inventions. . . . But it is significant that the German inventive genius, which in the past was somewhat backward, is now developing at a rate which bids fair soon to place the German beyond the need of English models. . . . But it must not be forgotten that the German imitation is not as a rule inferior in all respects. In the matter of artistic finish it is often—one may say, as a rule—decidedly better.

Nearly a century later, Ferguson talks about Japan in much the same tone. He writes, "Japanese companies begin with foreign technology, progress to internal development of process technology, and then move to internal product development and basic R&D. . . . Japanese producers are moving from low-priced consumer goods and 'clones' to high-performance, high-value-added business and industrial products."

Williams and Ferguson are strikingly similar. Logically, if a company is behind the state of the art, it cannot help beginning with imitation or clones-making. Examples are abundant. Thomas Edison began his light bulb research by imitating European precedents. Henry Ford began with reverse engineering of the French Renault model. American fine-chemical companies began by emulating German dye technologies. Therefore, it is no mystery that both Germany in the nineteenth century and today's Japan began with imitation.

Since Ferguson sees the strength of the Japanese information systems industry in the vertical alliances of a few *keiretsu* groups, he proposes that American and European companies emulate this peculiar type of industrial organization. Nearly a century ago, Williams gave a similar policy recipe to British industrialists. Williams said, "To the extent to which a foreign country shuts out our goods from her markets, to that extent should we penalize her goods in our market. Then, we must federate the Empire, in the most practical way—the way of commerce. At present we are losing our grip on our own colonies and dependencies, which are steadily falling into the hands of the Germans." Note that Williams also proposed an industrial federation to block a target country. Again, there is no conspicuous difference between Ferguson and Williams.

Why are their arguments so similar, even though Ferguson developed his own logic by focusing only on the information systems industry today, possibly without knowing of Ernest E. Williams? An explanation may lie in essential similarities between today's information systems industry and the nineteenth century dyestuff industry.

Germany, after imitating British and French precedents in artificial dyestuff technology in the late nineteenth century, controlled artificial-dye-technology–based derivatives such as photochemicals, pharmaceuticals, processed foods, synthetic fuels, and explosives. With those derivatives, Germany achieved quantum leaps in the optical, agrichemical, medical, aircraft, and rocket industries. This is a classical example of the "techno–food chain" of Inman and Burton.

Today, the United States has replaced England, and Japan has replaced Germany. Even with respect to *keiretsu,* Japan resembles Germany. As John J. Beer noted in his *The Emergence of the German Dye Industry,* "German dye producers felt they could no longer afford the luxury of competing with each other. They would have to eliminate all waste and avoid all duplication in their efforts to undersell their newly arisen rivals. The merger agreement between the Hoechst-Cassela-Kalle combine and the Agfa-Bayer-BASF syndicate went into force."

The Structural Bases for America's Erosion in Civilian Technology

"Techno-revisionism" and "techno-containment" illustrate the predominant view of the United States toward the Japanese technological threat. The United States has been increasingly irritated by the aggressiveness of Japanese firms' technological behavior in both the world market and the U.S. domestic market. Apart from Japan's rise as a technological superstate, other reasons may also account for American irritations, two of which are structural in nature:

1. In 1958 and subsequent years, the United States overreacted to the "Sputnik Shock" and put the nation's best and brightest into the military-related aerospace/computer fields, thereby drying up human resources for civilian technologies. This later contributed to the so-called industrial hollowing of the 1970s.
2. As technological advances have taken place, the demarcation between military and civilian technologies has increasingly become blurred so that the U.S. concentration on military technologies will have a crippling effect unless it guarantees spillover of civilian technology into military technology.

Understanding the first of these causes requires examination of the generational changes in American science and technology policy. The second cause is best understood through a review of the diversity of definitions of high technologies.

1. The "Generation Theory"

There are three generations of post–World War II American technological policymakers. The first generation maximized the use of civilian technology for military purposes. It was in fact a testament to the success of "spin-on" effects. The second generation skewed valuable national resources, human as well as physical, into military-oriented programs, thereby drying up resources for civilian sectors. Lacking commercial technological expertise, the third generation employed strong legal measures against the competing countries, particularly Japan, and could not reorient resources to bootstrap once-declining civilian sectors at home. The discontinuity of policies among these three distinctly different generations thus confused U.S. technological policy, military as well as civilian.

During World War II, the tradition of the National Research Council (NRC), which was created by Woodrow Wilson in World War I, was carried over to establish the National Defense Research Council (NRDC) in 1940 and the Office of Scientific Research and Development (OSRD) in 1941. The Nazis' Blitzkrieg, and the full exploitation of scientific and technological fruits for war purposes, forced the United States to take strong measures. Under Vannevar Bush's presidency, the OSRD commissioned major military research efforts, of which the most famous were nuclear energy research, an embryo of the army's Manhattan Project, and radar detection research conducted at M.I.T.

It is well known that the OSRD's successful missions were dependent on an interplay among government, industry, and university. For the purposes of the war, the global preeminence of American manufacturing technology helped the most. For example, Britain's magnetron, a microwave generator for radar, was simplified and manufactured by one of American's vacuum tube manufacturers, Raytheon.

After the war, Bush and other leading scientists and technologists advocated the creation of a government-supported organization for the enhancement of science and technology for peaceful purpose, that is, to maintain technological preeminence in private sectors.[5] However, Capitol Hill looked unfavorably upon their ideas on the grounds that scientists and technologists would acquire excessive political power. After long congressional debate, a law was passed in 1950 to create the National Science Foundation (NSF), which was limited to basic science and robbed of more important applied missions. With that, the first generation, like Vannevar Bush, Robert Oppenheimer, Karl Compton, and many others faded away from influential positions in American policy-making.

In 1949, the Soviet Union exploded an experimental atomic bomb, ten years in advance of American expectations. More shockingly, in 1957 the Russian Sputnik was successfully launched into orbit on October 4, ahead of America's Vanguard project (a navy project).

A month later, mindful of crisis fears, Dwight Eisenhower appointed James R. Killian, the first postwar M.I.T. president, to head the newly created Presidential Science Advisory Committee (PSAC), whose primary assignment was to direct America's military and related projects. In response to the Sputnik shock, Killian advised Eisenhower to create the National Aeronautics and Space Administration (NASA), the Advanced Research Projects Agency (ARPA) of the Department of Defense, the National Defense Educational Act (NDEA) of 1958, and the Federal Council for Science and Technology, and he reshuffled military missile projects.

Leading these new policy institutions, the second generation of America's science and technology policymakers climbed the ladder to the government's high-ranking posts. They differed from the first generation in that they were principally administrators or educators rather than great scientists or technologists. Their main concern was to contend against Russian military technology in the midst of the Cold War. As reflected in the enactment of the NDEA, America vacuumed the best and brightest into defense research, thereby drying up human resources for the civilian sectors.

Serious results became evident in the late 1970s, when America's industrial productivity declined for the first time. Before this, in 1971, President Nixon announced the formulation of the New Economic Policy, in which he declared the nonconvertibility between U.S. dollars and gold, which eventually led to the floating exchange rate regime.

The two oil shocks, in 1973 and 1979, dealt serious blows to the American economy immediately after the "Nixon Shock," causing the traditionally profitable American auto industry to begin to decline. The small, fuel-efficient Japanese cars quickly slipped into the American market and won the strong enthusiasm of American consumers. The American auto industry had been in a golden age for a half-century; since the turn of century, the brightest graduates of engineering schools had entered into this industry. However, as discussed above, the federal and defense programs made by the second generation of policymakers resulted in a shift of precious human resources exclusively into the aerospace industry and the military-contract divisions of corporations.

Given the threat by foreign competition, trade problems gave birth to the third generation of policymakers. In 1974, U.S. trade law experienced the first major revision since 1934. A stronger clause on retaliatory actions against unfair foreign trade practices was added. Local content actions and price-dumping suits called for tough American negotiators. They constitute the core of the third generation policymakers, who are dealing with foreign competitors to defend U.S. national security and industrial competitiveness.

The backgrounds of the policymakers of this generation lie in legal or policy administration, not science or technology. Thus, their focus is not on practicing useful policies to stop the decay of American technology at home, but rather on accusing foreign contenders of unfair business practices. The Toshiba-COCOM incident, the Super Article 301 negotiation, the FSX (Japan's next support fighter project) controversy, and the Structural Impediment Initiatives (SII) have all been battlefields for the third generation of policymakers against Japan.

2. From the "Spin-Off" to the "Spin-On"

The process of U.S. industrial hollowing was aggravated by the 1973 oil shock, which caused the world price of oil to multiply four times. However, if the Soviet Union had not been another hegemonic power with overriding military supremacy, as demonstrated by Sputnik and related missile technologies, the second generation would not have funneled so much of the nation's physical and human resources into military technology. In that sense, the hollowness of American industrial technology did not result from the oil crisis per se, but from the international politics of the Cold War. In other words, America's industrial hollowness was a result of policy choices, not of natural decay.

Industrial hollowing revived survivors of the second generation, spurring them to develop new ideologies. During the 1970s, when many criticized federal contracts for defense-related technologies, saying that they would invite "gold plating" or "white elephanting" at corporations, namely the waste of money for unnecessary R&D, the second generation hit on a useful policy ideology, the "spin-off" theory. They argued that huge federal defense programs would spill over into the civilian sectors and elevate the level of America's industrial technology, thereby contributing to the society at large.

However, industrial hollowing came much faster than the spillover effects, leading the second generation to formulate another new policy concept, called "dual-use" technology (DUT) or "spin-on" effects. DUT and "spin-on" both refer to the spilling of civilian high technology into military applications. Such civilian technology is called a DUT and its vector of cause and effect is the reverse of "spin-off" technology.

With these two concepts, the second generation of policymakers tried to capture foreign technologies in civilian use, in particular Japanese technologies, for they would have serious impacts on U.S. national security. A logical corollary of these arguments is that federal support should be provided for civilian technology that has dual-use functions, as these are allegedly vital to American security. Department of Defense programs, such as high-definition television, Sematech (a semiconductor consortium), US Memories, and the very-high-speed integrated circuit project (VHSIC), were justified under this rationale.

However, the above rationale has a fatal flaw, since one can never be certain which technologies will be DUTs. Suppose, for example, that semiconductor technology is classified as a DUT, but its development largely hinges on a wide variety of consumer applications, making it impossible to federally fund all the related areas of application. The resulting infeasibility of imposing rigorous federal spending accountability can lead to willful oversights, political maneuvering, and nepotism. This type of mismanagement can misdirect precious resources, contribute to the depletion of civilian technologies, and further exacerbate industrial decline.

The Rise of Japan by Emulous Power

When one nation is contained by another, a natural reaction is to build a similar counterblockade with the help of allies, or to nullify containment by suggesting friendly interdependent cooperation. C. Ferguson, feeling that the U.S. information systems industry is blocked by Japanese *keiretsu*, proposes the first option. Japan has continuously chosen the second option, namely, technological cooperation with the United States. In 1980, Prime Minister Ohira and President Carter signed the Japan–U.S. Treaty of Scientific and Technological Cooperation, which was renewed in 1988 at the Toronto Summit.

However, there remains the danger that interdependent cooperation in the area of technology can act as a collective "witch hunt" to encircle a target country. Ironically, because Japan and the United States are tightly bound in an interdependent relationship, the United States cannot help moving to encircle Japan's high technology. Before getting at this point, let us see what high technology really means.

1. What Is High Technology?

The phrase "high technology" has received popular attention, but debates on high technology are often shallow due to the lack of a clear definition of what high technology really means. For example, economists are prone to see high technology in terms of their favorite variable, namely, money. They define high technology as something that requires a large amount of R&D expenditure. Along this line, international cooperation achieves legitimacy because financial burden sharing helps solve the cost-overrun problems of most high-technology projects.

Politicians, on the other hand, tend to see high technology as related to military capabilities and national power. This view also has validity in the civilian sphere since a monopoly over a given dual-use technology critical to military purposes gives a country a strong hand in international relations. This fear led the United States to urge Japan to participate in the SDI project and to try to prevent the transfer of aerospace technologies as part of the FSX project.

The above two characterizations are macroscopic and do not touch on the internal or microscopic properties of high technology. One micro definition states that high technology introduces a new product through hybridization of two or more radically different technologies. Such hybrid mingling of different technologies often involves a traditional technology and a frontier one. A good example is the digital watch.

Another micro definition sees high technology as a radically new technology that will change the power balance of an industry. When a new technology is first introduced, it is difficult to assess its market potential, so that it is usually rejected by the established sectors of an industry. A good example is the introduction of transistors. When transistors were invented, opinions about their market potential differed between the vacuum tube manufacturers, such as GE and Westinghouse, and the electronic instrument companies. The former group rejected transistors, and the latter group accepted them, which resulted in a shift of power in the electronics industry. Namely, the principal makers of transistors turned out to be lesser-known companies like Texas Instruments and Motorola. This peculiar characteristic of high technology helps a minor player in an industry overthrow the major players: this can occur literally overnight, and thus create a new power regime in an industry.

The third micro feature of high technology is that the boundary between science and technology increasingly becomes blurred, as can be seen in the cases of biotechnology and superconductivity. This property is the grounds for the abovementioned economic definition of high technology, since large R&D investments are necessary to explore scientific foundations.

Given these characteristics of high technology, one may draw conclusions about their political implications. If we admit the economists' view that high technology requires huge R&D investment, we are compelled to hold the view that high technology will facilitate interdependent relations among nations. This argument is the prevalent rationale adopted by the G-7 Summit countries, which usually support international scientific and technological joint projects as a symbol of productive international cooperation.

However, high technology also involves "hybridity," and the successful hybrid mingling of different technologies generally occurs on an abrupt, breakthrough basis. This makes international agreement on budget appropriations difficult to justify for some unrealistic and uncertain projects. For these reasons, a country should develop technology independently.

This independent and self-financed effort naturally works to destroy existing international relations. Suppose that a country within an international cooperation scheme attains a technological breakthrough. This country may overthrow all other countries, leading to the breakup of an international cooperative scheme.

This is a technological version of the famous paradox of what the advocates of the complex interdependence thesis call the "vulnerability of interdependence." This paradox does not become a problem until a leading country attains technological preeminence and other countries enjoy their roles in the international division of labor. However, when a high-technology breakthrough topples such a leading country, interdependence in turn serves to stimulate collective "witch hunts." This often takes the shape of collective encirclement of a target country as a violator of international harmony. In this process, a country making a breakthrough is "contained."

2. Three Prerequisites for Successful Emulation

During the height of the Cold War, the United States generally enjoyed technological preeminence, both civilian and military. Japan was a semi-peripheral country whose primary assignment was to supply vacuums to the U.S. market. In this technological division of labor, the United States and Japan have been tightly bound to each other for their mutual benefit.

The United States lost preeminence in civilian technology for its own reason, which stemmed from the political nature of the Cold War, and Japan rose by attaining the hybridization of high technology. Because these two things happened simultaneously, the preceding U.S.–Japan bilateral interdependence could become a means to contain Japan. Unless the United States has access to Japanese civilian technologies, it cannot maintain military superiority, even in the post–Cold War era.

How did Japan become a technological superstate? It was no miracle. Thanks to its defeat in the Pacific War, Japan's military research was banned, so that the nation's best and brightest were mobilized into the manufacturing of civilian products. This was the opposite of the human resources policy shift of America's National Defense Educational Act of 1958.

Second, Japan could emulate American technologies, including quality control, by manufacturing captive products for the U.S. market. These included black-and-white and color televisions, tape and video cassette recorders for American broadcasting stations, and fuel-efficient small cars for American consumers. Third, Japan modified what it learned from American products. The just-in-time (no parts inventory) system is a good example. This is a case of bridging Japan's traditional approach of organizing the parts suppliers in a vertical way to the application of American car-assembly technology. This represents "hybridity" between a newly transferred technology of car assembly and Japan's traditional management style of purchasing auto assembly parts. In short, Japan's technological success lies in emulation.

Several preconditions are required for successful emulation to enhance national power. The first is that a nation should be integrated politically. If political integrity has not been achieved, national consensus for the diffusion of advanced technology is difficult. Moreover, economic support that encourages the diffusion of technology will not be forthcoming.

The second precondition is that the socioeconomic system should be almost the same as that of the countries from which the technology is emulated. The elements of a socioeconomic system to be copied include market style, corporate organization, education, and industrial structure. Without such an infrastructure in common, transferred technology will not penetrate so quickly into a recipient country.

The third precondition is that a recipient country should maintain a unique culture or tradition that will be conducive to later improvement of imitated technologies. Since this third quality may contradict the second qualification, it must be examined further.

No country can increase its national power only by imitating foreign technology. If it only produces goods that are exactly the same as those of other countries, superior foreign products will easily penetrate into the domestic market unless excessive protectionism or a strong import-substitutional policy is pursued. However, if a country can graft something different or something new onto the copied technologies, it stands a good chance of surpassing the donor countries. This is the heart of international technological emulation.

Japan's success in high technology was based on these three preconditions. First, since 1955, when the Liberal Democratic party and the Japan Socialist party were set forth, Japan has enjoyed political stability, which has left industrialists free to concentrate on economic recovery and technological enhancement. Second, after the occupation army, which was predominantly American, landed in Japan, Japanese socioeconomic institutions became Americanized. Thus there was no social barrier to the assimilation of American industrial products. This helped accelerate the clone-making of American products in post–World War II Japan. Third, as shown in the case of the just-in-time system, Japan maintained the Japanese way of doing things. This is in part the basis of the revisionists' thesis.

Some product areas in which Japan currently enjoys world preeminence are those in which Japan's unique culture or social institutions determine product quality. Therefore, it will be difficult for other countries to compete with Japan in those product areas, for they do not share the same cultural or societal conditions. Of course, if they develop a new type of product to meet their own cultural or social requirements in the future, they will have advantages over Japan.

Take the examples of laser printers, fax machines, or liquid crystal displays. With these products, Japanese consumers have a strong "voice" on the issue of product quality, and they strongly demand incessant improvement in quality. The Japanese use a mix of Chinese characters and phonetic letters, and reproduction of these requires higher-speed printing and more dot-matrix density than is required for simple alphabetical characters. Another example is a semiconductor chip. Japan's long popular history of using abacuses paved the way for the adoption of the lightweight electronic abacus, namely, the portable calculator, which later bootstrapped a new C-MOS semiconductor market. With this energy-saving C-MOS chip, Japan controls almost the entire lap-top personal computer market of the world. Japan's superior positions in the civilian technologies are corroborated by R&D statistics.

According to the 1985 data, Japan was placed at the top with respect to the GNP share of private R&D expenditures (2.19 percent), while American and West German shares were 1.45 percent and 1.71 percent, respectively. However, in terms of absolute amounts, according to the 1987 data, American expenditures for private R&D amounted to $60 billion, and Japanese counterparts amounted to $43 billion.

This does not indicate that U.S. activities in developing civilian technologies surpass those of Japan, because most U.S. private R&D involves government research contracts. For example, according to the 1988 data, 62.4 percent of the U.S. federal R&D research budget was for defense contracts, amounting to $33.8 billion, and a good portion of it would have gone to private contractors, while 47.6 percent of Japanese government's R&D research went to university research, amounting only to $5.8 billion. Therefore, in terms of pure expenditures spent by private sectors for research and development, Japan probably surpasses the United States.

Although Japan spends a large amount of money for private R&D, it imports more technologies from abroad than it exports to the world. The current export/import ratio is between 0.8 and 0.86 (according to the 1985 and 1986 data), and this is one reason why Japan is still accused of being a technological free-rider. For example, the recent Nikkei/Gallup survey indicates that some Americans (18.7 percent) feel uneasy about future American competitiveness and economic strength, and a majority of them (62.0 percent) believe that Japan is a technological free-rider. More Americans (74.7 percent) believe that Japan only imports foreign technologies and does not transfer its own; and more than one-third (36.7 percent) of Americans foresee that technological containment of Japan will occur from the United States.[6]

It is obvious that Japan's technological strength is not comprehensive, but is very limited, reflecting the areas in which Japan has successfully achieved fair emulation. However, these limited areas are currently most profitable areas, and they often occupy critical points in what Inman and Burton call the "technological food chain." What the world fears about Japan is exactly this, not that Japanese technologies are strong in every field. Therefore, unless Japan proposes a new policy in recognition of this fear, Japan will eventually be contained. This invites the question of which policy options are left for Japan.

Japan's Technology Agenda

Any external policy should be formulated by considering at least four points: (1) the ultimate policy objective; (2) the nature of the world order; (3) the grand strategy; and (4) specific means.

In diplomacy, the ultimate policy objective is national survival and the prosperity of the people. The same is true for technology: namely, the ultimate policy objective is also survival and the prosperity of technological actors, that is, private firms. Since technological survival and the prosperity of firms hinge on the ability to emulate, the ultimate objective of Japan's technological policy is to maintain these capabilities.

At present, American high-tech power has not completely deteriorated in all areas. However, U.S. hegemony in technology has ceased, and the United States can now be regarded as "ordinary." There are two other centers of technological excellence—Germany and Japan. They are not equal; each has its own merits and demerits. By taking advantages of its own strengths, each can exert influence in the international technological arena.

Cultivating new markets in Western and Eastern Europe and reconstructing East Germany will absorb German technological efforts for some time, containing Germany within Europe. Unless the United States and Japan aggressively enter into European markets to compete with Germany's interests, there will be no serious technological confrontations between Japan and Germany or between the United States and Germany in the near future.

One point is clear—Germany will achieve the status of a technological superpower. And, if Germany begins to transfer technologies to East European nations, it will partially fulfill one important prerequisite of a techno-hegemon, namely asymmetry. Moreover, future German technologies may become pervasive in Eastern Europe, including the Soviet Union. Perhaps Germany will take the Russian position as the techno-hegemon in the former COMECON region.

Japan's grand strategy is formulated against this background. Four-tiered, it is, more precisely, a two-plus-two strategy. The first two tiers of the strategy are cognitive and epistemological in nature. They are not action oriented; rather, they are conceptually illuminating and reveal general guidelines. On the other hand, the second two tiers are very much oriented toward the action of setting forth new policy paradigms. They demand a drastic change in current policy directions.

The first tier of the grand strategy is the tacit acceptance of Germany's vested interests and her technological dominance in East and some West European markets. Since much effort must be spent to cope with technological frictions with the United States, Japan should avoid extra disturbances with Germany in unknown territories. Joint ventures with German firms might be a good policy alternative for Japanese firms in these areas. The U.S. market is still the most profitable and secure for most Japanese firms.

The second tier of the grand strategy is to set a new policy paradigm—crisis management as opposed to crisis prevention. So far, Japan has been devoted to crisis prevention in its effort to cope with technological confrontations with the United States. Therefore, Japan has adopted a low-key, accommodating posture in technological relations with the United States in order to avoid excessive frictions.

When the United States accused Japanese firms of dumping color televisions in the U.S. market in 1968, Japanese manufacturers complied by establishing production sites in the United States in 1971 and by setting export quotas in 1977. Japanese auto manufacturers followed suit in the late 1970s and 1980s in the face of U.S. charges of unfair trade practices. Furthermore, the Japanese government established a voluntary restraint agreement for auto exports in 1980. In the area of military technology, when the United States demanded access to Japanese military-related technologies that were embargoed by the three principles on arms export, the Nakasone Cabinet relaxed the rule in 1983 and made an exception, allowing the transfer of military technology from Japan to the United States.

These actions indicate that Japan has attempted to prevent a clash with the United States in technology, both civilian and military. However, the potential for conflict is much worse because of the nature of high technologies in the technological food-chain, in which one key technology controls all others. Therefore, the crisis prevention principle is no longer realistic. Japan needs a clear policy of "crisis management," acknowledging that technological crises are inevitable.

1. "Techno-Detente"

Vigorous business activities by private firms in search of technological emulation lead to increased independence that helps repair economic relationships. If an external force does not intervene, this firm-level spontaneous adjustment should be effective.

However, if one of the governments intervenes to protect technological supremacy, techno-containment policy is a natural response. If a foreign government undermines the laissez-faire, self-adjusting nature of international techno-emulation, what should be the general principles of Japan's policy? First, it should be based on the expectation that other countries will try to narrow Japanese firms' international business activities. Second, the policy should try to avoid stimulating protectionism abroad while breaking up overseas containment trends. Third, it should maintain a domestic environment that encourages international emulation so as to avoid the parochial mentality that "made in Japan is always the best." In the meantime, if Japan feels contained by the United States, there could be a short-sighted reaction based on nationalistic sentiment and fear of isolation from the international community. Technological parochialism would lead to the loss of Japan's emulous power. We should never allow such a reaction. Avoidance of xenophobia is an absolute imperative.

Taking these three principles into account, I propose a policy of "techno-detente." This is the third tier of the game strategy. By "techno-detente," I mean a confrontational alliance between Japan and the United States. According to the second tier of the grand strategy, crisis management, this is not typically a friendly alliance, but a confrontational one based on crisis. Perhaps this might be criticized as discouraging healthy competition of technology among firms, both domestic and international.

However, I would counter that healthy free competition is achievable only when strong contenders, or, simply put, enemies, respect and seek to emulate each other, that is, when technological parochialism or arrogance is minimized. Therefore, if overseas contenders fade from the scene, healthy free competition can no longer be maintained. In this very sense, paradoxically, techno-detente guarantees a free technological competition. The legitimacy of the policy of techno-detente lies in this rationale.

Domestically, Japanese firms are fiercely competing with each other. Competition sometimes occurs within the *keiretsu* groups and sometimes between the *keiretsu* groups, depending upon the technologies. If one firm introduces a new product or a new technology, other competitors quickly emulate it and all firms stand on the same frontal line in a technological race. Techno-detente envisions something similar among Japanese firms and their American counterparts. However, many doubt that a true "borderless" competition among Japanese and American firms is possible. Why?

First, despite the slogan of the "borderless" era, "borderlessness" thus far involves only impersonal elements such as information, economic goods, or technological know-how. People are not moving freely across borders, so that there exists a nationalistic border within people's minds. To them, Japanese firms are Japanese and American firms are American. Techno-nationalism, techno-revisionism, and techno-containment all stem from this mindset. Therefore, before the intermingling of Japanese and American firms occurs in a truly borderless fashion, they will collide with each other.

Second, as the U.S.–Japanese Science and Technology Cooperation

Treaty of 1988 shows, competitive schemes between governments presuppose the authority of the contracting sovereign parties with national borders. Although the 1988 treaty is better than nothing, it is far from effective in stimulating cross-border emulation. The reason rests in political culture.

Any specific means for techno-detente cannot escape from the reality that there is a political border. Therefore, the means should aim at something contradictory: remove the border, but leave it where it lies. A national border can help retain emulous power. In fact, the contradictory difficulties associated with the implementation of the specific means for techno-detente are related to the dialectical nature of emulous conditions.

It is a contradiction that techno-detente requires both the removal and existence of the border. Because of this, there is no clear-cut answer to the question of how Japanese firms should expedite this grand strategy. The most plausible tactic might be something like the "let-a-thousand-flowers-bloom" approach. This is the fourth tier of the grand strategy. This approach aims at widening the channels of bilateral technological interaction between two countries at the private level. Joint ventures, employment of American workers, on-the-job-training and education of American engineers, direct capital investments, coproduction in the United States, etc., are all desirable.

Why at the private level? The answer is simple: it is only the private sector that can easily go beyond national borders. They cannot completely escape from nationality, but firms can behave more freely than the public sector. Moreover, they are the main actors engaged in emulation.

Since private firms do not spontaneously take an open-door policy for their key technologies, the Japanese government must assume responsibility in implementing the "let-a-thousand-flowers-bloom" approach. However, government policy should seek to encourage the desirable behavior of firms indirectly and should avoid direct coercion since this would destroy a good competitive environment.

Examples of how to facilitate this approach might be to (1) form an award committee composed of industrialists and academics, both Japanese and Americans (similar to the Deming Award Committee, which selects the company that has practiced the most successful quality control on the shop floor); (2) give a sizeable grant to the companies or persons who have devised and implemented the most effective scheme for widening technological interactions between Japan and the United States (for example, American Honda Motors or NUMII, a GM-Toyota joint venture, could be candidates); and (3) publicize this award internationally.

2. *"Soft Hegemony"*

Since the "let-a-thousand-flowers-bloom" approach encompasses inducements of many kinds, its overall effectiveness will continuously fluctuate. In order to compensate for this volatility, we need to enhance Japan's political leverage. Without sufficient political leverage for Japan, the United States will not agree with techno-detente. This is because most Americans still believe that U.S. high technologies are superior.

If Japan is considered a political dwarf, her "let-a-thousand-flowers-bloom" approach cannot be effective. The urgent need to enhance political leverage is obvious, but the question is, how can we do it? Here I propose a new concept, "soft hegemony," as a strategic concept for achieving this end.

In the past, political hegemony has been won by mobilizing hard resources, such as military capabilities, economic wealth, or technological assistance. By asymmetrically dispersing such resources, a hegemonic country could influence the behavior of the follower countries. A hegemon could then achieve an ordered, hierarchical international system at its disposal and reign over it.

In the theory of political power, these hard resources are called the "political base." However, the behavior of political actors can also be influenced by the so-called soft resources such as intellectual persuasion, psychological threats, or flattery.

In international politics, power resources have been viewed predominantly in terms of hard resources, simply because the international system was often transformed by war, in which military capabilities backed by economic strength played a decisive role. Since the end of World War II, however, the role of military capabilities has changed significantly. Although they were deployed in local wars, these wars themselves did not affect the balance in the international system during the entire Cold War period.

Cold War military capabilities functioned principally as a deterrent force to maintain the stability of the bipolar system. Then, a role shift from military to economic capabilities occurred with the advent of detente. As the advocates of complex interdependence argue, economic power has increasingly played a primary role in stirring the international system. But, in terms of the nature of the power base, nothing has changed, because both military and economic capabilities are the same in nature: that is, they involve hard resources.

If an argument based on soft resources is extended to the level of international politics, there emerges a new concept of "soft power." Joseph S. Nye, Jr., writes,

The changing nature of international politics has also made intangible forms of power more important. . . . Power is becoming less transferable, less coercive, and less tangible. . . . Co-optive power is the ability of a country to structure a situation so that other countries develop preferences or define their interests in ways consistent with its own. This power tends to arise from such resources as cultural and ideological attraction as well as rules and institutions of international regimes. The United States has more co-optive power than other countries.[7]

Whether the U.S. is a soft-power giant is worth debating, but the importance of soft power itself is not questionable.

How can Japan gain soft power? Currently, Japan has neither an internationally acknowledged ideology nor a worldwide-penetrating culture. But as Richard Rosecrance puts it, Japan is a trading state. Moreover, she is a technological state, too, where two conspicuous technologies, namely manufacturing technology and environmental and/or energy-saving technology, enjoy world preeminence. Among these three kinds of Japanese preeminence, trading power and manufacturing power are classified as types of hard power, so that they would not help Japan elevate its soft-power capability in the post–Cold War era. Therefore, let us focus on the third area, that is, environmental and/or energy-saving technologies.

Today, environmental issues such as deforestation, greenhouse effects, ozone holes, desertification, and the loss of biological diversity are becoming more and more globalized. As Jessica Tuchman Mathews puts it,

The assumptions and institutions that have governed international relations in the postwar era are a poor fit with new realities. Environmental strains that transcend national borders are already beginning to break down the sacred boundaries of national sovereignty, previously rendered porous by the information and communication revolutions and the instantaneous global movement of financial capital. The once sharp dividing line between foreign and domestic policy is blurred, forcing governments to grapple in international forums with issues that were contentious enough in the domestic arena.[8]

Japan is a leading country in both environmental legislation and technology. Admittedly, Japan is not a political superstate. But even as a political dwarf, Japan might be able to gain political leverage if it more actively engages in the international politics of the global environment, departing from hitherto passive attitudes of following a conservative course taken by the United States, the United Kingdom, and other industrialized countries. It is quite noteworthy that Germany recently showed, at the 1990 Houston Summit, a more assertive stance with respect to the global environment. If Japan plays a major role in singlehandedly giving her superior environmental and/or energy-saving technologies to countries who are seriously suffering from both security and economic threats caused by deforestation, desertification, acid rain, etc., Japan would be able to fulfill two prerequisites to becoming a "soft hegemon," that is, a hegemon capable of exercising co-optive power.

These prerequisites are exactly the same as those necessary for hard-power hegemony. They are (1) asymmetry; and (2) the existence of followers. The requirement of asymmetry would be fulfilled by asymmetrical donation of Japanese environmental and/or energy-saving technologies to the world, as well as its active engagement in environmental politics and support of environmentally suffering nations. The second requirement would be consummated when other major countries, including the United States, would, in due course, revise their conservative stances in environmental politics and follow the course laid out by Japan.

Notes

1. See Taizo Yakushiji, *The Dynamics of Techno-Emulation,* BRIE Working Paper no. 15, Berkeley: Center for International Studies, University of California, 1985.
2. On techno-parochialism, a similar argument is found in Michael L. Dertouzos, et al., eds., *Made in America* (Cambridge: M.I.T. Press, 1990), ch. 3.
3. *Foreign Affairs* 69, no. 2 (Spring 1990): 116–34.

4. Charles H. Ferguson, "Computers and the Coming of the U.S. Keiretsu," *Harvard Business Review* 4 (July–August 1990): 55–70.
5. See Vannevar Bush's famous report, *Science, The Endless Frontier: A Report to the President* (Washington, D.C.: Government Printing Office, 1945).
6. For more details, see "The Further Development of Natural Energy," *Nikkei Sangyo Shimbun,* December 6, 1990, 1, 6–7.
7. Joseph S. Nye, Jr., "Soft Power," *Foreign Policy* 80 (Fall 1990): 153–71.
8. Jessica T. Mathews, "Redefining Security," *Foreign Affairs* 68, no. 2 (Spring 1989): 162–77.

3. U.S.–Japan Macroeconomic Policy Coordination: Agenda for the 1990s and Beyond

Takatoshi Ito

Policy coordination is critical in the 1990s, an era in which no one country dominates the world economy or world politics. The United States, which had dominated for the previous four decades, became the world's largest debtor in the mid-1980s, while Japan emerged as the largest creditor. The last years of the 1980s witnessed dramatic changes in Eastern Europe and the Soviet Union. The change in the political stance of these countries, however, requires a major infusion of economic assistance from the Western world. In order to sustain a movement toward worldwide democracy, economic prosperity is crucial, and in order to sustain economic prosperity, macroeconomic coordination among the United States, Japan, and the European Community (EC) is critical. The need for funds, both for debt relief and for aggressive development strategies, comes at a time when the United States has lost dominance of the world economic order. A Marshall Plan in the 1990s is not possible without cooperation from Japan and Germany.

The experience with macroeconomic coordination among the Group of Seven countries (the United States, Japan, Germany, France, the United Kingdom, Canada, and Italy) during the 1980s provides an im-

portant lesson: policy coordination is an essential ingredient for successful management of the world economy, but could become counterproductive if misused. The macroeconomic coordination experience of the
Group of Five (later, Seven) countries during the 1980s can be conve-
niently divided into two periods, with no coordination occurring in the
first half and close coordination occurring in the second half. Each
regime involved both advantages and weaknesses in policy coordination.
In the first half, the United States essentially refused to admit that its
fiscal and monetary policy mix was causing twin deficits in both fiscal
budget and current accounts. On the other hand, it was widely acknowledged among economists that both tight U.S. monetary policy and growing fiscal deficits worked toward a higher interest rate and an overvaluation of the dollar.

The growing twin deficits became a major concern in the international
financial markets, and the rise in the dollar from the summer of 1984 to
the end of February 1985 was the last straw. The financial markets
became worried that the high level of the dollar might not be "sustainable" (Krugman 1985).

In Japan, one of the top priorities of the Ministry of Finance during
the first half of the 1980s was to restore balance in its government
budget. Tax brackets and basic deductions for income tax and inheri-
tance tax rates are not indexed, so that the failure to adjust brackets for
inflation and real growth resulted in a gradual reduction of deficits.
Although the Japanese government was concerned about growing trade
surpluses, they thought that U.S. policies were primarily responsible.

U.S. policy seemed to make a shift in early 1985, partly in response
to the growing concerns of the financial markets and trading partners
and partly because of a reshuffling among cabinet members in the second
Reagan administration. After James Baker became secretary of the Treasury, interventions in the foreign exchange market was reinstated for the
first time in three or four years.

In 1985, a change in U.S. policy was welcomed by major trading
partners, especially Japan and Germany. The Plaza Agreement on September 22 was a symbol of cooperation among the Group of Five. The
dollar, which had been declining since late February, accelerated its fall
after this agreement.

Despite the correction of the misalignment of exchange rates in 1986
and 1987, trade imbalances did not go away immediately. The lag

seemcd to last much longer than the usual theory suggested. The delayed response in pricing behavior among exporting and importing firms may be explained by diverse exchange rate expectations (Ito 1990) or rational wait-and-see strategies of the firms in a period of uncertainty (Krugman 1989; Dixit 1989a, 1989b). It was also discovered that the Japanese manufacturers actively engaged in extensive "pricing to market," while the U.S. manufacturers did not (Marston 1990). Whatever the explanation, the implication is the same: a prolonged misalignment is harmful to the economy.

This observation strongly suggests that policies should be coordinated to avoid prolonged fluctuations in exchange rates that amount to misalignment. Some economists recommend "target zones" to avoid misalignment (Williamson 1985; Williamson and Miller 1987; Krugman 1988).

Policy coordination to keep the U.S. dollar low continued during the difficult period when trade imbalances apparently did not go away. Frequent meetings of monetary authorities from the Group of Seven (and later the Group of Ten) countries reaffirmed their commitment to improving exchange rate management. There appeared to be an explicit target zone (Funabashi 1988; Ito 1989).

The trade imbalances finally started to respond to the exchange rate changes after two years. Japanese surpluses began to decline in 1986 and U.S. deficits also declined in 1987. The imbalances have decreased significantly since then. It is likely that the Japanese current account surplus came down to just about 1 percent of GNP for fiscal year 1990, partly due to the oil price hike in the summer and fall of 1990. The adjustment of the U.S. current account has been slower than the Japanese counterpart. However, if the pace of deficit reduction is maintained, an accumulated debt would be within the "sustainable" size. (This assessment is not based on rigorous econometric work, but on simple arithmetic and extrapolation.)

However, the movement of current accounts in both countries became asymmetric in 1991. The size of the surpluses more than doubled in Japan, while deficits shrank further in the United States. There are several reasons why Japanese surpluses increased in 1991. First, some part of a sharp decline in current accounts in 1990 was due to transitory factors—such as contributions to the multilateral (allied) forces during the Gulf War. Second, gold investment accounts distorted the official

Figure 3.1   U.S.–Japan Current Accounts in U.S. Dollars

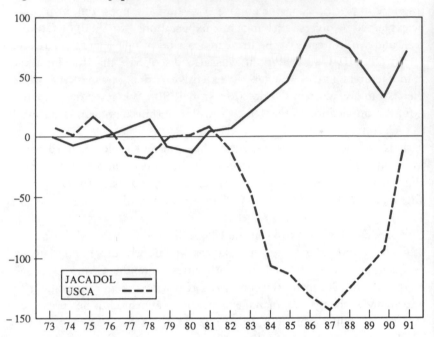

statistics on trade into and out of Japan. Third, the real exchange rate of Japan has depreciated since 1987.

As a result, we have seen the rise and fall of trade "imbalances" in the 1980s. Figure 3.1 shows the current account surpluses (or deficits) of Japan and the United States in U.S. dollars. Figure 3.2 shows the same graph in ratio to the respective GNPs. Both figures, in particular the GNP ratio, show the trade imbalances finally disappearing by the end of the 1980s. It appears that the trade imbalances are heading toward a soft landing.

However, policy coordination emphasizing exchange rate management is not necessarily the full answer. It is strongly suspected that inflation of asset prices in Japan from 1986 to 1988 was caused by a monetary policy that tried to keep the yen from appreciating "too much." After the initial success in depreciating the dollar by the Plaza Agreement, the monetary policy was switched to prevent too much yen appreciation in 1986. This policy continued until 1988 by lowering the official discount rates and money market rates. Stock prices and land

Figure 3.2 U.S.–Japan Current Account/GNP

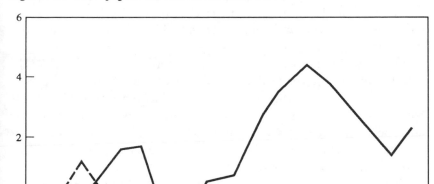

prices soared in the same period. General inflation was prevented only by the dramatic decline in oil and import prices. Hence, it is important to investigate the costs of coordination from the viewpoint of trade-off between external and internal objectives.

What are the lessons of this experience for the future? I will put forward several proposals for the 1990s.

Policy coordination is not a panacea. Prudent domestic fiscal and monetary policy has to be established as the basis for effective international policy coordination. There are two major concerns in U.S.–Japan policy coordination: a lack of fiscal discipline in the United States, and a tendency toward Japanese monetary expansion in the case of rapid yen appreciation.

When the key currency is running a large current account deficit, the international monetary system is potentially unstable. One way to retain confidence in the U.S. dollar is to establish an institution that would discourage the United States from succumbing to the temptation to issue debts that could be redeemed by inflation. The international monetary system should require the United States, or any other country in the Group of Seven that runs a current account deficit over a certain threshold, to issue government bonds denominated in foreign currencies. This is my first proposal.

The second proposal is to establish a "moving target zone." The target zone experiment in the second half of the 1980s was generally successful. However, when the target zone has the reasonably narrow band necessary to make it meaningful, frequent revisions of the ceiling and floor levels are necessary as fundamental variables change. Revisions can be made either in the form of automatically sliding ceilings and floors or in the form of contingency plans.

Third, the Japanese monetary authorities should make the Bank of Japan more independent from the Ministry of Finance, both in the legal sense and in the practical sense. The monetary policy-making process should be more transparent, while potent policy tools should keep monetary policy effective. The independence of the central bank from the Ministry of Finance is important, as it would relieve the central bank from the constant pressure to ease monetary policy (or to delay the timing of an official discount rate increase). More concretely: the provision of law that subordinates the Bank of Japan to the finance minister should be abolished; the practice that ex–Finance Ministry officials alternate with the central bank elite for the post of governor of the Bank of Japan should be ended; and the short-term treasury bill market should be expanded to allow open market operations. To this end, the transactions tax for near-maturity long-term bonds should be abolished.

I will now support the above remarks by considering five topics: the costs and benefits of policy coordination; the misalignment of exchange rates and trade imbalances; "coordination" after the Plaza Agreement; costs and benefits of the target zone after the Louvre Accord; and proposals for the future.

1. Policy Coordination, Benefits, and Costs

Those who are in favor of policy coordination among major industrialized nations make two arguments. Both are based on the fact that, in an interdependent world economy, policies in one country influence its trading partners' economies.

The first argument cites a welfare improvement among countries when the spillover effects on each other are taken into account. The logic is similar to that of "mutual backscratching." If the government of a country takes an action independently, maximizing its own welfare but disregarding spillover effects, the results for all countries are less than optimum. Take, for example, stimulative policies at a time of global recession. If such policies are uncoordinated, the world outcome falls short of full recovery because the beneficial effects of well-intended national efforts spill over into other countries, while the costs are borne by the initiating country alone. The initiating country, therefore, is unlikely to make a maximum effort. With coordination, spillover effects can be reciprocated so that the level of efforts will increase to "internalize" spillover effects.[1]

The second argument for coordination is to prevent a government from being induced to take a short-sighted policy, an action that is most likely for governments facing political difficulties. Hence, international policy coordination becomes a "discipline device." According to this argument, at times governments are not well intended even for their own citizens in that they may adopt policies that are politically favorable in the short run but economically harmful in the long run. For example, a policy stimulus such as an injection of fiscal expenditures or an expansion of money supply might increase employment and produce faster growth without much inflation in the short run. However, if the policy stimulus continues, people will expect the inflation rate to rise, and the change in expectation will result in actual inflation, and may even result in run-away inflation. Hence, the beneficial policy causes harm in the long run.[2]

If there is policy coordination to restrain inflation effectively, say by use of a target zone for exchange rates or multilateral macroeconomic "surveillance," this kind of short-sighted policy may be prevented. Another obvious example of such a policy is the beggar-thy-neighbor policy, which depreciates the exchange rate in order to push exports to trading partners. Depreciation of the currency may be produced by expansionary monetary policy or contractionary fiscal policy, if not by a blatant, direct intervention in the foreign exchange market. If the exchange rate is managed, this type of policy will be prevented.

Despite these advantages, policy coordination may be challenged on several grounds. There is a theoretical possibility that coordination may be counterproductive. When a government pursues its own objectives, disregarding its own economy's benefit, coordination may allow this government to escape punishment. In other words, coordination may weaken a discipline device that is effective in the absence of coordination (see Rogoff 1985). Suppose that a government puts a higher weight on the value of employment relative to inflation, compared to the private sector. The expansionary policy would cause currency depreciation, which would accelerate inflation that comes from domestic reasons anyway. The currency depreciation would enhance the costs of a policy that is undesirable from the private sector's point of view. However, if the target zone is in place, the trading partner is obliged to take measures to stabilize the exchange rate, that is, to take an inflationary policy itself. Thus, an automatic discipline device is nullified by the exchange rate target in this case.[3]

There are two other, more practical arguments against coordination. First, even if all theoretical assumptions are in favor of coordination, the "true" model of the world may not be known by the policymakers (see Frankel and Rockett 1988). In fact, they typically believe in different models. For example, suppose that the United States and Japan agreed on macroeconomic targets, such as inflation and the growth rates of the two countries. The United States may use the Federal Reserve Board's Multicountry Model (MCM) to calculate its own policy for the good of a coordinated G-2 world, while the Japanese government may use the Economic Planning Agency's (EPA) world model to derive its own policy package. Both models also take into account the other countries' policies. However, if the MCM and EPA models have different structures (or structural parameters), then coordination may result in failure. Even if the models agree, but the models are not "true," mistaken policy may result. Frankel and Rockett (1988) conducted simulations using the representative macroeconomic models of the world and came to the conclusion that welfare is improved by coordination in only about half of one thousand cases that are possible combinations of what is believed by governments and what is truth. This exercise shows that it is important for governments to agree on the models their cooperative efforts are based on and to make sure the models are good ones.

The second practical point is that even if coordination is desirable, and even if recognition of the true model is possible, the magnitude of benefit from coordination may be small. Oudiz and Sachs (1984) estimated the gain by the United States as being a "utility equivalent of one-half percentage point of GNP in each of the next few years." Their estimate was about the same for Germany and Japan.

In summary, for various reasons, in the second half of the 1980s many economists started questioning the axiom that policy coordination is a good thing (see Feldstein 1987). This, however, does not mean that they all are against coordination. Instead, the majority opinion among economists is that although policy coordination is basically beneficial, there are many caveats. With these arguments for and against coordination in mind, let us now review U.S. and Japanese policies in the 1980s.

2. Misalignment of Exchange Rates and Trade Imbalances, 1980–85

In the first half of the 1980s, the trade deficit of the United States grew in concert with Japan's increasing trade surplus. Many economists pointed out then that there were two major, connected problems behind the trade imbalances: the exchange rate misalignment during the period 1981–85, and macro Savings-Investment (SI) imbalances. Let us examine these issues.

First, observe that a country's production has to be consumed by the private sector, invested by the private sector, expended by the government, or exported. Imports are also added to consumption, investment, or government expenditure. Hence, trade balance, which is the difference between exports and imports, is the difference between what is produced and what is absorbed domestically—that is, the sum of consumption, investment, and government expenditure. Note that government expenditures are, at least partly, financed by tax revenues—that is, by transfer of resources from the private sector to the government—and the transfer does not affect the absorption calculation. The difference between tax revenues and government expenditures is defined as the fiscal surplus or deficit. On the private sector side, an introduction of taxes will change national product into disposable income (defined as national product less taxes). Thus, the difference between the disposable income less consumption—that is, savings—and investment defines the S − I balances of the private sector. In summary, the following relationship must hold: [4]

$$
\begin{pmatrix} \text{Domestic} \\ \text{saving} \\ \text{less} \\ \text{investment} \end{pmatrix} + \begin{pmatrix} \text{fiscal} \\ \text{surplus} \end{pmatrix} = \begin{pmatrix} \text{trade} \\ \text{surplus} \end{pmatrix}
$$

I shall refer to this as the identity equation. The 1980s started with high inflation caused by the second oil crisis in 1979–80. The United

States introduced a tight monetary policy in 1979 that did not start to ease until the summer of 1982. A cautious stance (that is, one that kept interest rates relatively high), in fact, continued until 1984. On the fiscal side, the Reagan tax cut of 1981, combined with his military buildup, caused a large government deficit. The tax cut, both on earned income and on capital gains, was based on the belief that a reduction in rate would stimulate willingness to supply more labor and more capital investment so that the level of tax revenues would increase. Supply side economics was proven wrong: the level of tax revenues did not rise with the rate cut; the Reagan administration created one of the worst fiscal deficits in U.S. history; and lower capital gains taxes did not cause investment to rise enough to compensate for the rate cut. Moreover, the decrease in the private savings rate, with investments being relatively stable, certainly contributed to increasing trade deficits.

By the identity equation, a government deficit along with negative private net savings necessarily means a trade deficit. Without an increase in private savings or a decrease in private investment, fiscal deficits necessarily mean trade deficits. The trade deficit was in this sense mainly a macro phenomenon. The other side of the current account (that is, trade accounts plus transfers) deficit is the capital inflow that finances the payment of net imports.

The identity equation shows that correction of trade imbalances requires correction of macro balances as well as trade barriers. In fact, tariff and nontariff trade barriers and cultural or noncultural discrimination against foreign commodities were certainly declining in Japan throughout the first half of the 1980s. Hence, trade barriers (that is, protected, closed markets created by regulations and unique trading practices) cannot be the heart of the trade balance problem. Instead, serious proposals should attempt to correct the savings-investment balances in the two countries.

From 1983 to 1986, when the twin deficits soared, the rise in U.S. interest rates was relatively moderate despite large fiscal deficits. This was due to large capital inflows, particularly from Japan, which helped meet the fund demand from the U.S. government sector. As a result, real economic growth remained high. In that sense, U.S. economic performance was not bad, given the U.S. fiscal and monetary economic policies then in place. However, it was unfortunate that discipline was not imposed on the U.S. government: the high interest rate would have choked the economy and induced a policy switch had the capital from

Japan not been allowed to flow as freely as it did. Since Japan and Germany were reluctant to raise interest rates to match U.S. interest rates, capital flows were unable to stop dollar appreciation. Their export industries enjoyed a boom from the U.S. policy mix.

The combination of expansionary fiscal policies and restrictive monetary policies led to a relatively high interest rate, which attracted capital from abroad. The strong dollar in turn hurt the competitive position of U.S. exporters in world markets. The dollar appreciation from 1982 to the beginning of 1985 became known as "misalignment." The key to understanding the misalignment was the capital flow. Since the pressure to purchase the dollar-denominated assets was so strong, the self-correcting mechanism of trade deficits leading to currency depreciation did not occur. Many economists believe that the pressure of the capital inflow to the United States was caused by a particular U.S. policy mix, while the U.S. government maintained that the strong dollar was a result of world investors' preferences. The U.S. government rejected Japanese and European criticism on the cause of the misalignment. Thus, international coordination was not possible in the first half of the 1980s.

Since Japan had higher overall productivity growth and lower inflation than the United States, the yen in the long run should have appreciated against the dollar. Suppose that the exchange rates of 1973 and 1980, the two years when the Japanese current account was nearly zero, were, respectively, the "equilibrium" exchange rate at the time, and then extrapolate the line to 1989. The "equilibrium" exchange rate is shown by the broken line in figure 3.3. Since the exact place of the "equilibrium" exchange rate is not known with much confidence, this line should be regarded as an approximation. However, deviations of the actual exchange rate (the solid line) from the equilibrium rate were so spectacular that there can be no mistake that there was a misalignment.

A rapid increase in the U.S. current account deficits from 1982 to 1985 finally compelled the U.S. government to change its position. In particular, the dollar appreciation from the summer of 1984 to the beginning of 1985 was regarded by many as a "bubble." There were no fundamental reasons for a sharp appreciation. At the same time, the question of whether the level of the dollar was "sustainable" became the focus of attention, both in the academic world and in the political arena. Krugman (1985) strongly argued that the prevailing level of the dollar was not sustainable since the resulting trade deficits imply a snowballing of external deficits.

Figure 3.3 Yen/Dollar Rate

¥/$

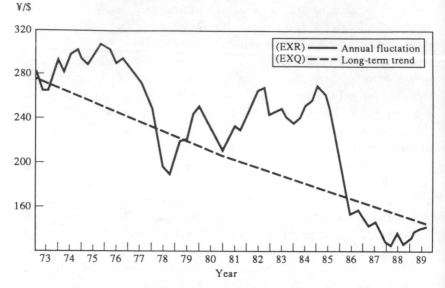

A switch from an internationally uncoordinated policy to a coordinated one was inevitable. The actual change in policy had to wait until James Baker III assumed the position of treasury secretary from Donald Regan. On September 22, 1985, ministers of the monetary authorities of the Group of Five gathered in the Plaza Hotel, and they announced agreement on policy measures designed to push down the value of the dollar. This was the beginning of policy coordination in the second half of the 1980s. From the Plaza Agreement of September 1985 to the Louvre Accord of February 1987, there were frequent negotiations, and strong steps were taken to correct the overvaluation of the dollar (see Funabashi 1988). The process was a remarkable success, as the dollar depreciated vis-à-vis the major trading partners' currencies by 60 percent in a year or two. For example, the yen was traded at 263 yen per dollar in February 1985; by August 1986 it stood at 152 yen per dollar. Figure 3.3 reveals that the overvaluation of the dollar quickly disappeared. Feldstein (1987) deemphasized the success of coordination represented by the Plaza Agreement by pointing out that the degree of dollar depreciation from February 1985 to September 1985 (pre-Plaza) was as large as that from September 1985 to April of 1986 (post-Plaza). However, it was a surprise in the market that the dollar depreciated so quickly after the Plaza Agreement, and it was through policy coordination that the pre-Plaza correction of the bubble was continued.

In summary, the second half of the 1980s saw a soft landing of trade imbalances, aided by a decline in oil prices (to be discussed in the next section). As we all know, the success of the Plaza Agreement and the Louvre Accord led to the appropriate exchange rate. U.S. government deficits finally started to decline, and investment in Japan increased rapidly. Many were optimistic that the macro imbalances would continue to shrink in the 1990s.

3. "Coordination" after the Plaza Agreement, 1985–87

A closer look reveals that the road to coordination was not as smooth as it appeared. In the three months after the Plaza Agreement of September 1985, the Bank of Japan, along with the Federal Reserve and other central banks, sold dollars. However, the pledge in the Plaza Agreement to bring down the dollar was quickly rescinded in March 1986, when the Bank of Japan "reversed" the direction of intervention to slow down the pace of yen appreciation, a fact forgotten in many recent writings. The Japanese monetary authorities, with possible pressure from the business community, decided that the yen had appreciated enough and that more appreciation would cause serious damage to its export industry. In fact, there were indications of an "appreciation recession" *(endaka fukyo)*. This conflicted with the U.S. view that more appreciation of the yen was needed to bring down the size of the trade imbalances between the two countries.

My study (Ito 1987) of the intradaily exchange rate movement indicates that more than half of the appreciation from January to August 1986 was caused by oil price decline. During this period, the yen appreciated approximately from 190 yen per dollar to 150 yen per dollar, while oil prices declined from 28 dollars to 10 dollars (later bouncing back to 18 dollars). If the oil price decline, which is a change in the "fundamentals," built major pressure to appreciate the yen in the first half of 1986, the policy to counter the pressure by intervention was inappropriate. Intervention is most effective if it is unsterilized—that is, if foreign exchange intervention is done without affecting domestic money supply—and the unsterilized intervention amounted to an increase in the money supply. (This point became more important in 1987, as I will explain in the next section.)

The rift between Japan and the United States concerning whether the yen should appreciate more continued until the fall of 1986. In the meantime, the yen appreciated to the level of 150 yen per dollar despite the Bank of Japan's intervention in support of the dollar (selling of the yen).

4. Costs and Benefits of the Target Zone after the Louvre Accord

The Louvre Accord of February 1987 is usually regarded as having initiated the system of a "target zone for exchange rates." The communique indicated that the monetary authorities of the Group of Seven countries wanted to maintain exchange rates at around "the current level." Although there was no mention of a range in the written accord, it was widely reported that the monetary authorities at least talked about a range, if they did not agree on one.

A target zone, sometimes called a reference range, is a band of exchange rates that the central banks aim to maintain by adjusting fiscal and monetary policies, including interventions. Theoretically, it has been shown to contain exchange rate fluctuation by influencing the expectations of the market participants (Krugman 1988; Williamson 1985; Williamson and Miller 1987).

However, the theoretical work on this concept assumes that the chosen target zone is a maintainable one from the viewpoint of "fundamentals." Put differently, the target zone is assumed to include the "equilibrium" rate. The possibility of the target zone being broken is not accounted for in the theoretical model.

The target zone was reportedly revised twice in 1987. In April, the lower boundary for the yen decreased (that is, in the direction of a stronger yen), and then, after Black Monday in October, further yen appreciation was allowed. (See figure 3.4, which is adapted from Ito [1989], and see also Funabashi's [1988] documentations.) There are two possible explanations: first, that the revisions were triggered by newly available news; second, that the target zone was set incorrectly and

Figure 3.4 Yen/$ after G5

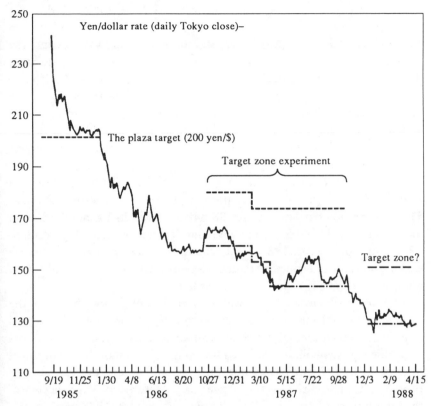

proved impossible to defend, so that a revision became necessary. The latter possibility is more likely.

Changes in foreign exchange reserves are reasonably good indications of the degree of intervention. The increase in foreign exchange reserves for Japan indicates the purchase of the dollar by the yen. During the year 1987, the foreign exchange reserves increased from $42 billion to $81 billion. This increase of almost $40 billion was quite extraordinary, since the reserve increased only $16 billion in 1986 and only $17 billion in 1988. Even though many dollars were purchased, the target zone, and the revised target zone, were not defended. This strongly implies the second explanation.

What were the side effects of heavy interventions? Interventions were most likely unsterilized, because money supply (M2 + CD) growth unexpectedly accelerated in 1987. It had an 8.9 percent (over the past four quarters) growth rate in the first quarter of 1987, and it rose to 11.4 percent by 1988. Moreover, the increase went way beyond the Bank of Japan's own "forecasts." As money supply growth accelerated, the market interest rate declined.

The year 1987 is also known as the year of "asset inflation"; the national average of land prices (as officially posted by the Land Agency) increased 25 percent during 1987, the largest increase in fifteen years. In particular, the land price in Tokyo increased 69 percent, the largest increase since the survey started in 1971.

The link between the target zone and asset price inflation provides an example of how policy coordination might affect domestic economy. The asset price inflation of 1986–88 did not result in a general inflation of consumer prices. However, wholesale prices dropped 9 percent in 1986 and 4 percent in 1987, while consumer prices virtually stayed the same. That consumer prices remained constant when they should have gone down can be taken as a sign of inflation.

Another problem in 1987 was that trade imbalances between the United States and Japan did not diminish. The "J-curve effect" suggests that changes in trade balances lag behind exchange rate changes. However, this lag was believed to last something like six months or, at most, one year. The two-year delay prompted debates among economists and provoked U.S. congressional criticism. U.S. frustration was reflected in the adoption of "Super 301," a provision attached in 1988 to a general trade bill requiring retaliation against "unfair practices" (by U.S. definition).

There are several explanations for the significant delay in trade balance adjustment. First, Japanese exporters adjusted their prices to compensate for the exchange rate changes so that the dollar-denominated prices in the United States would not change much (Marston 1990). This pricing behavior, known as "pricing to market," reflected the exporters' efforts to retain their shares of the market. Second, when firms suspect that exchange rate changes might be temporary, their production and marketing decisions employ a "wait-and-see" strategy until the new equilibrium rate is established. Hence, during the waiting period, there is too little change in location of production or prices of imports to cause a large correction of the trade imbalances (see Krugman 1989; Dixit 1989a, 1989b). Third, the survey data show that the market participants did not expect the sharp exchange rate changes until they had happened. They tended to expect that a large exchange rate would be temporary (see Ito 1990a). For example, a week after the Plaza Agreement, when the rate was 225 yen per dollar as compared to 240 yen per dollar the previous week, the average market participant expected the dollar to go back to 230 yen per dollar in six months.

This line of argument shows that it is important to prevent a large "misalignment." Hence, a target zone may be a good idea. However, once a large misalignment (say, dollar overvaluation) has occurred, a temporary opposite misalignment may be needed to bring the rate to an equilibrium value (Krugman 1989). A cumulative mistake cannot be corrected by bringing the level to equilibrium. From this viewpoint, it would have been a better policy to let the yen appreciate to the level of 120 yen per dollar as early as 1987. The target zone implemented by the Louvre Accord was right in the long run, but it failed to consider the large misalignment of the preceding five years.

5. Proposals for the 1990s: The United States and the International Monetary System

Let us summarize the lessons of the 1980s for policy coordination. The first half of the decade exemplifies the danger of noncoordination in terms of the undisciplined fiscal policy of the United States. The second half of the decade provides an opposite example: the establishment of a target zone resulted in too expansionary a Japanese monetary policy, which contributed to asset price inflation.

The danger of no coordination is all too clear from the U.S. experience in the first half of the 1980s, which produced historic deficits that affected all other major trading partners in one way or another. This experience proves that policy coordination is in general beneficial. However, it must be used carefully. First, policy coordination must be closely tied to appropriate domestic policies. Second, when a target for coordination seems to produce undesirable side effects, it should be revised promptly.

The International Monetary Order

In order to maintain discipline in monetary and fiscal policies, various devices other than policy coordination should be introduced. Since the dollar is a key currency, the trade deficits of the United States can become quite large if there is no automatic discipline device.[5] One discipline device is, of course, a target zone. However, a target zone has been convincingly shown to have its own limitations. Another discipline device is a type of Gramm-Rudman legislation that limits fiscal deficits and imposes automatic spending cuts. However, experience has shown that this will not be a reliable device unless there is a continuing desire for fiscal restraint in the U.S. Congress. A more radical reform would be to require the United States to issue foreign-currency denominated government bonds (similar to the so-called Carter bonds) when trade deficits (or net foreign assets) go beyond a certain threshold. This kind of commitment, which may be unpopular in the United States, will enhance the long-run economic welfare of the United States as well as its major trading partners. This also answers the asset settlement question discussed below.

In addition to creating a disciplinary device for U.S. government deficits, it is necessary to consider a fundamental institutional change in the international monetary system in order to prevent another episode of severe misalignment. The key currency country is now the largest net borrower in the world, and the United States will no longer be able to keep borrowing from abroad to finance government deficits in the 1990s.

This is the old question of what is an appropriate asset settlement for the key currency country. In the final stage of the Bretton-Woods system, European countries, notably France, insisted that the United States be willing to "settle" the debt caused by "dollar overhang" by selling gold in exchange for dollars. The question did not completely become moot after the floating exchange rate system came into place.

One possibility for a new international monetary order would be to use a basket (some kind of mix) of the dollar, the yen, and the ECU for foreign reserve requirements of the major countries. The same basket could be used as the unit of international borrowing by a debtor nation's government.

During the 1980s, there were other kinds of asset settlements. After being saturated by large holdings of U.S. government securities, Japanese investors diversified their portfolios by increasing shares of equities (most notably in 1987–88), direct investment, and real estate (1988–89). The purchases of Rockefeller Center, Firestone, and Columbia Pictures are only a few conspicuous examples of an alternative means of asset settlement in the era of deregulated capital movement.

Toward Institutional Harmonization

As barriers to international movements of goods and capital have been lowered, institutional harmonization, such as tax harmonization, similar antitrust legislation and implementation, etc., in addition to macro policy coordination among the major developed nations, have become important issues. For example, when traditional capital controls are abolished, capital taxation must be coordinated in order to eliminate the possibility that unilateral capital movements, induced by the differential in tax treatment, will disrupt the function of the world capital market. Traditional tax haven countries are all too small to be easily countered by, for example, interest equalization taxation of the major advanced countries. However, if a country as large as the United States decides to play such a game, the effect could be enormous.[6] Transaction costs have been lowered by technological progress in communication, so that it has become more important in the 1990s to harmonize tax treatment of world capital income and movement.

Other areas of harmonization include regulations regarding the banking and securities businesses (universal banking in Europe versus separation of the two sectors in the United States and Japan); antitrust legislation and implementation; government-business relations in Japan and Europe; and regulations on new financial products. It appears to be inevitable that these regulations and barriers will converge toward a uniform world standard, if only gradually.

One particular example of the area that needs to be harmonized is the lack of a short-term government securities market in Japan,[7] which causes at least two significant problems. The Bank of Japan cannot rely on open market operations as an important monetary tool. The central bank still uses direct loans with low interest rates to large banks to control the money supply. This practice is criticized by other countries as subsidizing Japanese financial institutions. (As a response to this criticism, the Bank of Japan expanded the list of institutions eligible for direct loans in 1990.) Second, foreign institutional investors shy away from the Japanese market because the lack of safe, short-term assets makes it hard to "park" funds when adjusting portfolios. For "internationalizing" the yen it is absolutely necessary to have a deep, short-term government securities market.

In order to create such a market, at least one of the following must be done: (1) transactions of middle- and long-term government securities should be exempted from the securities transactions tax; (2) "repurchase agreement" transactions should be exempted from the securities transactions tax; and (3) "near-maturity" long-term bonds should be exempted from the securities transactions tax. Many economists advocate these institutional changes. However, the Tax Bureau of the Ministry of Finance has resisted them.

6. Japan's Initiative in the 1990s

The role of Japan in enhancing the chance of better world economic management cannot be overemphasized. The United States had taken the initiative for economic and political innovation during most of the postwar period. However, the economic "size" of Japan and of a united Europe will match, if not exceed, that of North America. Without the cooperation of the financial powers of Japan and the EC, it will be impossible to implement new economic arrangements and initiatives, such as solving accumulated debts in Latin American countries, infusing capital in Eastern European countries and the Soviet Union, and, more generally, enhancing the functions of international organizations. Unfortunately, Japan's initiative in the sphere of economic relations in the 1980s has been disappointing. It was rare for Japan to take the initiative to help solve existing problems, such as trade conflicts, and to establish a new economic order, such as a new trade organization that strengthens the existing General Agreement on Tariffs and Trade (GATT).[8]

In the rest of this section, I will emphasize four categories of contributions that, I think, Japan should make in the future: (1) reassessment of policy coordination and the role of the Bank of Japan; (2) reform of Japan's political system; (3) initiatives in international organizations; and (4) initiatives in the U.S.–Japan bilateral relationship.

*Reassessment of Policy Coordination and the Role of the
Bank of Japan*

The Japanese monetary and fiscal authorities should reevaluate their priorities as they look toward the twenty-first century. First, recall that the policy to resist yen appreciation in 1986 and 1987 may have been counterproductive after all. In a sense, the policy favored exporters and land owners at the expense of import-consuming citizens and renters (through asset price inflation). Although it is unclear that this kind of judgment was actually made, it was an obvious byproduct of the target zone and of policy coordination. Second, if the trade deficits were to be reduced quickly (mostly for political reasons), the Japanese authorities could have employed a different policy mix. Namely, the monetary policy could have been tighter and fiscal policies could have been more expansionary. The IS balance (recall the identity equation) implies that the expansionary fiscal policies of 1986 and 1987 would have reduced the Japanese trade surpluses. I hope that lessons from the 1980s will contribute to better international policy coordination and domestic policy management.

The target zone concept should be modified if it is tried again in the 1990s. First, when it is tried again, participants should make certain that the range includes a correct short-run as well as long-run equilibrium level. Second, in the long run, the target should be adjusted to reflect changes in the fundamentals. However, revisions of zone ceiling and floor by steps may prompt speculative attacks, just as the fixed exchange rate has done. To avoid this, a "moving target zone" can be constructed using, for example, the interest rate differential. The moving target zone in 1987 would have looked like the one depicted in figure 3.5. (See, for details, Ito 1989.)

In order to assure the benefits of policy coordination, the independent role of the Bank of Japan should be strengthened. The fiscal authority of Japan is tied to the election cycle and is thus more susceptible to short-sighted goals. (Recall the example of a "not well-intended" policy presented in section 1 of this paper.) The Bank of Japan, if more independent, may be better able to pursue the goal of preventing (asset) price inflation. Some measures might be (1) to abolish the article that makes the Bank of Japan subordinate to the finance minister; and (2) to end the practice by which an ex–Finance Ministry official alternates with the central bank elite for the Bank of Japan governor post. For example, the practice can be changed so that major changes in monetary policy, such as official discount rate changes, are decided within the Bank of Japan before they are reported to the Ministry of Finance. More authority in foreign exchange market interventions may be given to the Bank of

Figure 3.5 Sliding Zone Experiment

Japan. This would avoid the political rift between the two authorities that often causes delays in implementing necessary changes.

Reform of Japan's Political System

It is often pointed out that Japanese economic power is not accompanied by political prowess. During the 1980s, Japanese policymakers, bureaucrats, and politicians alike, took little initiative in trade conflicts or policy coordination. The United States and Japan engaged in numerous negotiations, talks, and working groups, such as the negotiations for voluntary automobile export restraints; negotiations regarding beef and citrus imports; the yen/dollar working group; the Market-Oriented Sector Selective (MOSS) talks; the semiconductor agreement and U.S. retaliations for its violation; the Super-301 negotiations; and complaints about cellular phones and amorphous patents. Almost always, the United States "demands" that actions be taken by the Japanese, and the Japanese reluctantly comply or compromise only after a long delay and U.S. "threats" of retaliation.

I interpret this pattern of demand-and-compromise as a product of the Japanese and U.S. political systems. The Japanese position is determined by special interests, not economic principles such as the principle of competition and free market, which could be used to change policy. U.S. demands, or "foreign pressure," is virtually the only source of policy innovation. The Ministry of Finance and the Ministry of International Trade and Industries have skillfully used foreign pressures to break vested interest groups without politically humiliating them, since U.S. demands have still been viewed as political givens *(shoganai)*. This is probably due to inertia stemming from the occupation period after World War II, and to the fact that losing to U.S. government pressures, as opposed to domestic political competitors, is not considered a political loss.[9]

On the other side of the Pacific, blaming Japan has provided an easy way out of political troubles. The Democratic-controlled Congress and the Republican White House competed for political vantage by vying with each other in being tough against "unfair" trading practices. Even though the true cause for economic problems is known to be domestic, politicians tend to blame foreigners. For example, many economists, whether Japanese or Americans, have argued that a major cause of the U.S. trade deficits in the mid-1980s was large fiscal deficits, not Japanese "unfair trading practices," if they existed. Many in the U.S. Congress did not listen. Moreover, some in Congress justified the threats of retaliation against Japan as the only way to focus the attention of the White House on the seriousness of the trade debt problem. As a long-time world leader, the United States is not accustomed to listening to other countries, but instead acts as a policeman self-appointed to ensure free markets. Japan became a target partly because it seemed that Japan had succeeded in economic growth without employing full-scale "free market" principles.

The demand-and-compromise style of negotiation is increasingly viewed by the Americans as a shrewd delaying tactic of Japan (Prestowitz 1988), and is viewed by the Japanese as unwanted U.S. intervention in Japanese internal affairs (Ishihara and Morita 1989). It is dangerous to continue in this mode.

Moreover, to focus narrowly on the U.S.–Japan relationship is a fundamental mistake for Japan. It alienates the EC and weakens multilateralism by international organizations. In fact, European countries have repeatedly expressed concerns over U.S.–Japan negotiations on various issues, including the semiconductor agreement. From the long-run strategic point of view, Japan, along with the rest of the world, is much better off if political priorities are given to multilateral negotiations and agreements.

The Japanese political system, including bureaucrats and politicians, must change in order to avoid serious future trade conflicts. To break vested interests and to enhance consumer welfare, it should adopt some principles and should act according to them, not waiting for foreign pressure. Such a new principle might be dedication to consumer-oriented policies or to creating a society that could experience affluence. An important theme is to shift political priorities from "stability of business" (a code phrase referring to protection of vested interests, incumbents, and "in-groups") to "consumer welfare" (a code phrase for free entry and competition). Cases are abundant: the Daiten ho, a law restricting construction of large-scale retail stores; financial deregulations on deposit interest rates; and rice importation. It is important to have some slogan or principle to use against vested interest groups. The Maekawa Report had such a mission, but its recommendations were not well implemented.

Initiatives in International Organizations

International organizations and institutions such as the World Bank, the IMF, and GATT should be reemphasized. The cooperation of developed countries in a multilateral framework will be more important than ever, partly because the U.S.–Japan bilateral agreements have recently produced an antagonistic atmosphere, and partly because movement toward regionalism, spawned by EC 1992 and the North American Free Trade arrangement, may become a threat to the world trading system.

Japanese capital is a useful resource for international organizations. Some argue that Japan's large trade surplus—that is, its capital outflow—is an important source of development funds for Latin America and Eastern Europe. However, this argument mistakes results for causes. If productive investment opportunities exist, investment will take place, wherever the financial source is. Even in the latter half of the 1980s, Japanese long-term investment was more than trade surplus. However, this characteristic dramatically changed in 1991. Japanese long-term capital became an "inflow" despite relatively large current account surpluses. Basically, Japan appeared to have received dollars for investments in addition to having earned dollars through trade. This was just the reverse of the previous years, when the short-term capital movement became a huge "outflow." There are two ways to characterize this situation. Either Japan repaid borrowings by selling long-term assets abroad or foreigners withdrew short-term yen-dominated assets and bought long-term yen-dominated assets. A close examination (Ito 1993) reveals that the latter characterization is closer to reality.

It is important for Japan to think about what contributions it can make through international organizations. However, there are several constraints in this area.

First, Japan is underrepresented in most international organizations. Although the quota for Japan in the World Bank and the IMF is 6 percent, Japanese professional staff in each organization constitutes only about 1 percent, including those who are basically "on loan" from the Japanese ministries and the central bank, and, in the case of the World Bank, some Japanese firms. The situation is similar in the United Nations and other international agencies. There are several reasons for this underrepresentation, one of which is the lifetime employment system in Japan, which prevents those who want to return to Japan in midcareer from getting good job opportunities. Domestic as well as international job mobility must be enhanced. Another reason is that Japanese firms and the Japanese bureaucracy emphasize "general skills" (all-round generalists trained in various tasks and positions) rather than "professional skills." Hence, many who are judged useful in domestic terms cannot function adequately in professional positions in international organizations that require highly professional skills. Japan must accept and nurture professionals by treating and rewarding them better.

Second, the agenda for Japan is not well articulated. "Initiative" and "public relations" are not traditional traits of the Japanese political process. Many political decisions, including the selection of prime ministers, have been decided behind closed doors and by in-group consultations. The Japanese decision-making process itself is not "transparent," and as a result other countries become puzzled, cautious, and suspicious of Japan's intentions. This must change.

Initiatives in the Bilateral Relationship

U.S.–Japan bilateral trade negotiations in the 1980s produced temporary compromises but contributed to a long-term deterioration in the public opinion of each country toward the other. The semiconductor agreement and its aftermath, and the designation of Japan as an unfair trading partner in Super-301, created strong resentment in Japan. In the United States, the repeated pattern of U.S. demands and Japanese concessions, in addition to Super-301, yielded a perception among some of the American public that Japan's success is based upon unfair business practices. Since bilateral negotiations bear a political cost, as explained above, there needs to be a better institutional framework for resolving U.S.–Japan problems before they become politicized.

There are two steps to place the U.S.–Japan bilateral relationship in a wider perspective. First, Japan can pursue a leadership role in international organizations, such as the IMF, the World Bank, and GATT. Many difficult problems, such as lending to East European countries and former Soviet republics, cannot be solved through international vehicles alone. Japan and the United States have to take leadership in these organizations. Japan has not acted as a leader in the past. In order to avoid a frustrating bilateral relationship, Japan has to learn how to take a leading role in multilateral organizations.

Second, expanding the free trade zone beyond North America to include Japan must be considered. There are many obvious political and economic obstacles to such an arrangement, but the benefits of such an agreement would seem to outweigh the costs for U.S.–Japan relations. In the presence of the free trade zone, most questions about bilateral trade talks and conflicts become moot. Political energy and resources can be shifted from bilateral negotiations to leadership in multilateral international organizations and domestic issues. This would be a desirable change for Japan.

7. Concluding Remarks

To create a better world in the 1990s, Japan, the United States, and the European countries must better coordinate their macroeconomic policies and harmonize institutions. Japan must better express its agenda and stress international (multilateral) cooperation, rather than narrowly focus on the U.S.–Japan (bilateral) relationship. Both Japan and the United States have to put their own houses in order. Only when each country has put its house in order will policy coordination become productive. It is important in the 1990s that policy cooperation go beyond the U.S.–Japan bilateral relationship. Multilateral organizations and institutions, such as the IMF, the World Bank, and GATT, should be strengthened. Policy coordination in the area of exchange rate management and a free trade zone must be expanded beyond a two-country framework. For example, a Japan–North America (the United States, Canada, and Mexico) free trade zone should be seriously considered.

If these proposals are adopted, Japan, the United States, and the rest of the world would move toward a more prosperous world with fewer conflicts and confrontations.

Notes

I have benefited from comments on an earlier version by Fred Bergsten, Yoichi Funabashi, Robert Lawrence, and Edward Lincoln. This project has been partly supported by the National Institute for Research Advancement (NIRA) through the Japan Center for International Exchange (JCIE), and partly by a Ministry of Education grant (Monbusho Kagaku Kenkyuhi [No. 02630048]).

1. The situation can be understood as an application of the "prisoner's dilemma." A noncoordinated equilibrium is a suboptimal Nash solution, while a coordinated equilibrium is optimal. This line of argument was first proposed by Hamada (1976). See also other papers in Buiter and Marston (1985).
2. This argument is based on the framework of an "expectation-augmented" Phillips curve, which shows an inflation-unemployment tradeoff, and a political business cycles theory. For the former, see any intermediate macroeconomics textbook, and for the latter, see Ito (1990b).
3. The second example of undesirable coordination is the case where the government has a credibility problem (see Kehoe 1989). If the private sector suspects that the government might tax capital income in the future, investment will be less than optimal. The government does not have any way to

convince the private sector that a high tax will not occur in the future. The situation would be the same in the case of open economies with coordination. In the case of noncoordination, international competition would drive the capital tax to zero; otherwise, capital flight would have harmful effects on the high tax country. Hence, policy coordination that prevents capital tax competition is a bad idea.

4. The savings-investment balance approach can be derived from the two identities. First, recall the definition of GNP, $Y = C + I + G + X - M$, where Y denotes GNP, C consumption, I investment, G government expenditure, X exports, and M imports. The second identity is the household budget constraint, $Y - T = C + S$, where S stands for saving, T for taxes. By substituting out Y from the two equations and arranging terms, we obtain $(S - I) + (T - G) = (X - M)$, where $(S - I)$ is the private-sector savings and investment difference, $(T - G)$ is the government (fiscal) surplus, and $(X - M)$ is the trade surplus.

In the first half of the 1980s, the macroeconomic positions of Japan and the United States could be illustrated as follows:

	$(S-I)$	$+$	$(T-G)$	$=$	$(X-M)$
U.S.	$-$		$--$		$---$
Japan	$++$		0		$++$

5. However, theoretically this argument is not really a proof. See Krugman (1989, 115). Since dependence on imported essential goods in the United States is less than in other countries, the cost of default and of trade sanctions is lower for the United States. Thus, if the international community is less dependent on trade, it theoretically stops lending to the United States at a lower level of debt in ratio to GNP than for other, smaller counties.

6. Currently, interest income is not withheld by U.S. depository institutions whether a depositor is a resident or nonresident as long as it presents proper tax IDs. In contrast, interest income is withheld at the rate of 20 percent in Japan, regardless of the origin of the money (with an exception for other central banks and international agencies for the purchase of Japanese government bonds). The U.S. Treasury demands that withholding should be abolished. The Japanese Ministry of Finance takes the position that the current tax treaty institutes withholding of interest income, that the United States unilaterally waives the right to withhold, and that withholding is less costly in assessing tax liability.

7. There are several kinds of government securities in Japan: "treasury bonds" (TBs) or government securities with less than one-year maturities; "fiscal bonds" (FBs) or sixty-day revenue-smoothing securities; "middle-term" (five-year maturity) discount bonds; and "long-term" (mostly ten-year, and sometimes twenty-year maturity) government bonds with coupons. TBs are issued at discount by auction (for financial institutions, not for individuals) but FBs are mainly issued to the Bank of Japan (due to its low interest rate). TBs and

FBs are exempt from securities transaction tax, but middle-term and long-term government bonds are not. Hence, it becomes prohibitively expensive to trade middle-term or long-term bonds near maturity. The volume of TBs is not enough to form a deep market that can withstand open market operations by the Bank of Japan.
8. A notable exception is the Miyazawa Plan, advocating a scheme of helping heavily indebted countries. However, this was only recently replaced by the Brady initiative, which is very similar to the Miyazawa Plan.
9. The following jokes, on the same theme, highlight this kind of view: (1) A two-party system works in Japan, the LDP for big-business special interests versus the United States for consumers; (2) the United States Trade Representative (USTR) is the best consumer advocate one can get in Japan.

References

Buiter, Willem H., and Richard C. Marston, eds. (1985). *International Economic Policy Coordination.* Cambridge University Press.
Dixit, Avinash (1989a). "Entry and Decisions of a Firm under Uncertainty." *Journal of Political Economy* 97: 620–38.
——— (1989b). "Hysteresis, Import Pricing, and Pass-Through." *Quarterly Journal of Economics* 104: 205–28.
Feldstein, Martin (1987). "Rethinking International Economic Coordination." A lecture on the occasion of the fiftieth anniversary of Nuffield College, Oxford, October.
Frankel, Jeffrey A., and Katharine E. Rockett (1988). "International Macroeconomic Policy Coordination When Policymakers Do Not Agree on the True Model." *American Economic Review* 78: 318–40.
Funabashi, Yoichi (1988). *Managing the Dollar: From the Plaza to the Louvre.* Institute for International Economics, May.
Hamada, Koichi (1976). "A Strategic Analysis of Monetary Interdependence." *Journal of Political Economy* 84: 677–700.
Ishihara, Shintaro, and Akio Morita (1989). *"No" to ieru Nihon (Japan That Can Say "No").* Tokyo: Kobunsha.
Ito, Takatoshi (1987). "The Intradaily Exchange Rate Dynamics and Monetary Policies after the Group of Five Agreement." *Journal of the Japanese and International Economies* 1: 275–98.
——— (1989). "Was There a Target Zone?" In JCIF Policy Study Series, no. 14, June.
——— (1990a). "Foreign Exchange Rate Expectations: Micro Survey Data." *American Economic Review* 80 (June 1990): 434–49.
——— (1990b). "The Timing of Elections and Political Business Cycles in Japan." *Journal of Asian Economics* 1: 135–56.
——— (1993). "On Recent Movements of Current Accounts and Capital Flows of Japan." In T. Ito and A. O. Krueger, eds., *Macroeconomic Linkage:*

Exchange Rates and Capital Flows. NBER East Asia Seminar on Economics, vol. 3. University of Chicago Press.

Kehoe, Patrick J. (1989). "Policy Cooperation among Benevolent Governments May Be Undesirable." *Review of Economic Studies* 56: 289–96.

Krugman, Paul (1985). "Is the Strong Dollar Sustainable?" In *The U.S. Dollar: Prospects and Policy Options.* Federal Reserve Bank of Kansas City.

——— (1988). "Target Zone and Exchange Rate Dynamics." National Bureau of Economic Research, working paper no. 2481, January.

——— (1989). *Exchange-Rate Instability.* Cambridge, Mass.: MIT Press.

Marston, Richard C. (1990). "Price Behavior in Japanese and U.S. Manufacturing." NBER working paper no. 3364, May.

Oudiz, Gilles, and Jeffrey Sachs (1984). "Macroeconomic Policy Coordination among the Industrial Economies." Brookings Papers on Economic Activity, no. 1. 1–64.

Prestowitz, Clyde V., Jr. (1988). *Trading Places.* New York: Basic Books.

Rogoff, Kenneth (1985). "Can International Monetary Policy Cooperation Be Counterproductive?" *Journal of International Economics* 18: 199–217.

Williamson, John (1985). *The Exchange Rate System.* 2d ed. Institute of International Economics.

Williamson, John, and Marcus H. Miller (1987). *Targets and Indicators: A Blueprint for the International Coordination of Economic Policy.* Institute for International Economics, September.

4. Rule Maker of World Trade: Japan's Trade Strategy and the World Trading System

Kazumasa Iwata

1. Structural Changes in World Trade

Now that much of the military threat by Communist countries has disappeared, economic frictions between the United States and Japan could reemerge at the forefront of political debates. Notably, after the Gulf War Japan was criticized for its failure to play a stronger role in constructing a new world order. The failure to conclude the GATT Uruguay Round talks in December 1990 undermined the base of the multilateral free trade system and increased the risk of mounting protectionism in the forthcoming decade. It is of critical importance that Japan move to maintain the free trade system that has been the mainstay of Japan's remarkable economic success. Japan faces the challenge of transforming its trade policy from the reactive policy of the past to a rule-based policy conducive to construction of a new global and liberal trading system.

Looking back to the 1980s we can discern four remarkable structural changes that gave rise to major challenges to the world trading system. The first structural change was a marked tendency toward formation of regional groupings, while the globalization of market economies proceeded. Global market activity was facilitated by technological development in information flow and communication and by the conversion of Communist countries to market-oriented economies. But at the same time there emerged a strong tendency toward forming three regional groupings consisting of the extended European region, including the Eastern European countries; the U.S.–led region; and the Japan-centered Western Pacific region.[1] The advance of Japan and Asian countries in the past decade precipitated the move by the former two groups toward regional groupings.

Secondly, rapid technological innovation caused drastic changes in international competitiveness with regard to high-tech products. The high-tech industries are characterized by economies of scale and dynamic efficiency arising from large learning effects. The development of high-tech industries requires heavy R&D investment, thereby causing significant spillover effects on related sectors. The linkage externalities, coupled with large learning effects, lure governments to adopt strategic trade policies to "create" comparative advantages and to shift the profit from foreign firms to domestic firms under an oligopolistic market structure. The success story of Japan's industrial policy, though it was a product of specific historical circumstances, provoked some U.S. officials and scholars to advocate the industrial policy's promoting export and "managed trade" arrangements with regard to high-tech products: Tyson (1990) argues for extending bilateral sectoral arrangements such as the U.S.–Japan semiconductor agreement to multilateral managed trade arrangements.

The third change was the increasing role of intrafirm trade. In the 1980s there appeared a new wave of direct investment among advanced economies and some of the newly industrializing countries. The surge of direct investment by Japan in the United States and Asia after 1985 strengthened business linkages through capital movement and expansion of intrafirm trade.

U.S. multinational firms exported $71.3 billion to overseas affiliated companies in 1986, while importing $65.6 billion from them. These figures amount to 31.4 percent and 18.0 percent in total export and import, respectively. In the case of Japan, the shares of intrafirm export and import are larger than those of the United States; the shares of total exports and imports amounted to 32.0 percent and 26.0 percent, respectively, with the intrafirm trade balance being in large surplus

Table 4.1 Intrafirm Trade in the United States and Japan

	Total Value	Share in Total Export and Import
U.S. (1986)		
Export	$71.1 billion	31.8%
Japan	$3.6	13.8
Canada	$31.6	55.9
Europe	$19.7	32.6
Import	$65.5	24.4
Japan	$7.3	7.5
Canada	$29.8	38.3
Europe	$9.2	10.3
Japan (1986)		
Export	$97.9	32.0
North America	$64.9	54.1
Europe	$21.1	21.1
Import	$29.4	26.0
North America	$16.6	50.9
Europe	$3.8	22.5

($68.4 billion) in 1986. Notably, the intrafirm trade imbalance was marked in North American–Japanese bilateral trade (table 4.1).

Moreover, there exists a strong trend toward "competitive alliances" among big multinational firms. If we include international trade based on licenses and contracts on technology, marketing (distribution, sales, and use of brand names such as original equipment manufacturing [OEM] exports), and joint R&D in intrafirm trade, then about half of the international trade among advanced economies can be identified as intrafirm trade, broadly defined.

International factor movements are replacing international trade based on difference of endowments (interindustry trade), internalizing the adjustment costs of trade in goods and trade barriers. This leads to a smaller share of interindustry trade and expansion of intrafirm trade and establishment trade, the latter of which can be identified as trade in services. It may also internalize trade friction related to interindustry trade, because it creates employment and contributes to an increase in exports of the host country. Further, national interests will be diluted by the increased importance of foreign markets for multinational firms.

On the other hand, intrafirm trade may give rise to more intense friction over investment. It may also reinforce the tendency toward a more oligopolistic market structure of world trade. The increasing number of gray area measures, measures on the margin of free trade practices, supported by government intervention also serve to maintain an oligopolistic market structure. Further, if imports are dominated by intrafirm trade, this may constitute an obstacle to market access for foreign companies in the downstream distribution sector of the oligopolistic structure (Lawrence 1987). In addition, as international trade increasingly resembles trade in the domestic economy due to the increased mobility of production factors, the trade dispute becomes more closely connected with differences in domestic regulations and the issues of industrial organization. This points to the need to create a single market within a wider region or on a global basis by harmonizing domestic regulations, institutions, and law.

If intrafirm trade is carried out on the basis of a subdivision of the production process within multinational companies, it may lead to increased intraindustry trade. Intraindustry trade accounted for more than half of the trade in advanced economies; the exception was Japan, where half of imports is primary commodities, notably energy. The peculiarity of natural endowments and rapid structural change in production and exports worked to maintain Japan's intraindustry index at a low level. Notably, the self-sufficient processing structure played an important role in determining the share of intraindustry trade (Iwata 1991).

Dornbusch proposed managed trade agreements different from Tyson's, namely, to increase U.S. manufactured exports to Japan by 15 percent a year. He cites the low level of intraindustry trade as evidence of market closedness. Yet Japan's intraindustry trade index exhibits a marked rising trend for manufactured products since 1987. If the overall trade imbalance effect is adjusted, it rose to about 0.5 in 1989, which is close to the U.S. level and mainly reflects the increasing outward processing of manufactured products and the diversified demand for consumers' goods (table 4.2).[2]

A fourth structural change was the expansion of trade in services. The transformation toward a service economy in advanced countries

Table 4.2 Intraindustry Trade in Major Countries

	Intraindustry Trade Index (1989)		Estimation by Lincoln (1985)	
	All Products	Manufactured Products	All Products	Manufactured Products
U.S.	0.55	0.64	0.54	0.61
Japan	0.28	0.49	0.23	0.26
EC	0.85	0.91	—	—
non-EC	0.64	0.76	—	—
Germany	0.78	0.65	0.63	0.67
France	0.73	0.81	0.74	0.82

Source: MITI, Annual Survey on Trade in 1990, Lincoln (1990).
Note: *Trade imbalance effect is adjusted with respect to manufactured products.

reinvigorates trade in services. If we define trade in services as the sum of invisible trade (transportation, tourism, insurance, patents, royalties, and investment revenue abroad) and unilateral labor income transfer, we see that it expanded more rapidly than trade in goods in the 1980s. Since investment revenue is regarded as the reward for management services rendered by the home company to an affiliated company, it is included in trade in services.

Trade in services can be divided into three groups. One group consists of services splintered from the process of producing goods. The second group is trade in services accompanied by international movement of production factors; one type of this category is establishment trade (for instance, construction engineering and retail banking) and another is trade in professional services (e.g., the services of lawyers and accountants). Third is trade in services accompanied by international movement by consumers (for instance, tourism). Thus, trade in services is crucially connected to regulations and barriers on direct investment and international labor mobility.

In addition, trade in services embraces the services embodied in goods and production factors; intermediate service input is embodied in goods and can be included in trade in services. Japan has a deficit in trade in services if it is measured by figures listed in invisible trade, while the United States shows a large surplus, notably with respect to patents and royalties. But the picture changes if we adopt a broader definition of services that includes services embodied in goods. Both Japan and the

Table 4.3　Trade in Services: The United States and Japan ($ billion)

	Invisible Trade	Trade in Goods Total	Separated Trade		Embodied
World					
Export	752.0 (42.6%)	1767.2	—	—	—
Import	825.5 (47.1%)	1753.9	—	—	—
U.S.					
Export	143.3 (66.2%)	216.2	61.4*	228.6*	289.9*
Import	122.7 (36.3%)	337.8	16.7*	165.4*	182.5*
Japan					
Export	45.5 (26.2%)	173.6	31.9	122.1	154.0
Import	50.7 (43.0%)	118.0	18.0	79.1	97.1

Source: IMF, *Balance of Payments Statistics*, Sazanami and Urata (1990).
Note: * indicates the figure in 1982.
The estimates are separated, and embodied trades in service are derived from the input-output tables of Japan and the United States.

United States are net exporters of services (table 4.3). It may be noted that the embodied services take on a much larger share of trade in services than do splintered services.

This fact led Grubel (1989) to conclude that there is no need for a new round of negotiations on services. He finds that free trade in goods and free establishment trade are sufficient to cover trade in services; conceptually he identifies the splintered services as value-added embodied in goods. But services such as finance, insurance, and data banks' services are more and more disembodied from production of goods, and are traded independently from trade in goods.

These structural changes challenge the free trade system. The world economy is in the process of forming a single market, but there is also a drift toward regionalism and managed trade under an oligopolistic market structure. Trade issues become much more complex and more deeply rooted in different domestic institutions and regulations. A strategic trade policy increasingly looks attractive for obtaining monopolistic rent. Despite the globalization of market activity, there have emerged "trade wars" among regional groups based on strategic policy and institutionalized or judicialized protectionism. In addition, gray area measures under an oligopolistic market structure have been eroding the free trade system and replacing it with a managed trade system.

2. Main Shortcomings of the General Agreement on Tariffs and Trade (GATT)

When the GATT was established, though legally only on a provisional basis, it implied the establishment of an international institution to promote and maintain global free trade in the world economy; it brought about a big shift of trade policy from protectionism to commitment to internationally agreed upon rules and norms by the contracting parties. However, the norms and principles of GATT were undermined by challenges arising from structural changes and revived mercantilistic trade policies.

The GATT provides a framework of norms for the world trading system and a forum for negotiation. It also provides detailed codes of behavior for the participating countries in the form of legal rights and obligations, although the enforcement and compensation mechanism is not strong enough to solve all the trade disputes. This legal structure is significantly different from those of other international institutions like the IMF, the IBRD, and the OECD.

As norms we can mention nondiscrimination, liberalization of trade barriers, reciprocity in concessions, and multinationalism. The central norm is nondiscrimination. It guarantees competition among private enterprises on an equal basis in the international marketplace. When governments apply trade restrictions uniformly without regard to the origin of products, the efficiency of resource allocation will be secured through the market mechanism. In addition, the norm of nondiscrimination checks the tendency toward selfish and discretionary mercantilist trade policies.

The unconditional most-favored-nation clause, national treatment, and transparency are the rules and procedures based on the norm of nondiscrimination. The unconditional MFN commitments help to minimize the costs of rule formation as well as transaction costs at customs. They also serve to promote a generalization of liberalizing trade policy; they function as the "mutual insurance" (Patterson 1987) that the benefits of barrier reductions through negotiation will be secured by precluding trading partners from giving more favorable treatment to other countries.

Both the nondiscriminaton norm and the unconditional MFN procedure have, however, been undermined and modified in the process of pragmatic adaptation to changing circumstances. As a result, the GATT became a "troubled institution" (Jackson 1990) or even an "instrument of illiberalism" tending to protect the political interests of politicians and bureaucrats (Grubel 1989). The main shortcomings of the GATT can be divided into five categories: (1) insufficient coverage of GATT; (2) derogation from GATT norms; (3) increasing gray area measures outside the GATT; (4) lack of clarity on unfair trade practices in the GATT articles and the code agreements; and (5) lack of legal integrity and rule implementation of the GATT.

The negotiations at the GATT have traditionally focused on manufactured goods. The trade of agriculture was left outside of the GATT in the mid-1950s by the motion of the U.S. and EC. The U.S. acquired the waivers from the GATT under pressure from Congress based on the Agriculture Adjustment Law, while the EC strengthened protection of the agriculture sector by embarking on the Common Agriculture Policy (CAP). The turnaround of U.S. trade policy on agriculture products in the Uruguay Round talks collided with the EC's CAP, which constitutes the core of economic integration within EC countries.

The GATT traditionally paid scant attention to trade in services; rather, it tended to take up issues of the lowest denominator of the participating countries.

Revived nationalism and mercantilism became more pronounced after the 1950s. The first major attack on norms was the permission to establish the EEC, the EFTA, the free trade area agreements, and other regional agreements such as the U.S.–Canada Automobile Product Arrangements. There are now more than sixty such arrangements. Even today GATT takes an extremely lax stance toward free trade area formation and has not strictly monitored compliance with article 24, which requires for free trade agreements the liberalization of substantially all trade and less restrictive tariff barriers toward third countries.

The second attack on norms was the Multifiber Arrangement (Short-Term Arrangement in 1961, Long-Term Arrangement in 1962, Multifiber Arrangement in 1974, 1977, 1981, and 1986). This sectoral arrangement initiated institutional protection or managed trade, followed by more informal or bilateral arrangements on footwear, television, steel (worldwide export limitation in 1984), automobiles, and semiconductors. Although the MFA served to prevent more severe bilateral trade restriction on textiles, the GATT provided a framework of institutional protection that built discriminatory safeguards into the world trading system on a formal basis.

The third attack was the approval of special and discriminatory preferences for the trade of developing countries (General System of Preference). First proposed in United Nations Conference on Trade and Development (UNCTAD), the GSP was authorized by the enabling clause of the understanding at the Tokyo Round.

The fourth attack was the code agreements at the Tokyo Round. The conditional MFN was applied by the United States to the codes on subsidies and countervailing duties, government procurement, and technical standards. GATT legal arguments justified the U.S. stance on the first two codes.

Gray Area Trade Practices

The increasing number of gray area trade practices outside the framework of the GATT (249 in September 1989) demonstrates the ineffectiveness of the safeguard mechanism, as exemplified by the difficulty in reaching agreement on discriminatory applications, surveillance, time period of degressivity, and structural adjustment, as well as drawbacks in dispute settlement mechanisms. The GATT escape clause (article 19), which is a descendant of the U.S.–Mexico Reciprocal Agreement of 1943, is regarded by many governments as inadequate, so arrangements outside the GATT have been devised.

Measures such as the Voluntary Export Restraint (VER), the Export Restraint Agreement (ERA), the Voluntary Restraint Agreement (VRA), and the Orderly Marketing Agreement (OMA) can be regarded as selective safeguards against particular sources of imports, typically instituted as a compromise with protectionism. The VERs often lack transparency and easily accommodate political pressure toward protectionism. They evade national legal problems and GATT disciplines. The monopoly rent distributed to exporting firms seems to compensate or overcompensate for the loss incurred by the agreement. The consumers of importing countries suffer most from the higher price of imported goods, while domestic firms and politicians share the rent with foreign firms. In this sense the VER dominates tariff policy. It can be interpreted as a cartel agreement on profit sharing or as a reverse dumping practice endorsed by the governments. On the other hand, the Voluntary Import Expansion (VIE) can be regarded as export protection. Tyson (1990) advocates the VIE as a key element of rule-oriented managed trade, which may contribute to increasing trade by removing the market barriers stemming from unfair business practices.

Unfair Trade Practices

GATT articles pertaining to antidumping duties, subsidies, and countervailing duties lack clarity. The additional codes agreed upon at the Tokyo Round are haunted by ambiguity and contradiction. Antidumping laws and countervailing duties tend to be employed for the purpose of protecting domestic industry. Antidumping calculations of unfair prices is often difficult to implement, notably in the case of increasing-return-to-scale industry. Differences in economic systems, such as employment systems, add to the difficulty of correctly constructing cost. To a certain extent "unfairness" reflects differences in economic structure among different countries. If a structural change arising from the requirements of international trade is too rapid and costly, then the safeguards and antidumping duties work as a buffer to rebalance the burden of the costs of structural adaptation. If we accept this interpretation of unfairness, then what is needed most is international agreement on the application of the principle of national treatment in domestic competition policy, combined with support for structural adaptation and adequate compensation. Currently, structural adaptation relief is only available to developing countries through the World Bank, while compensation is limited to the suspension of GATT obligations (GATT article 23).

Lack of Legal Integrity and Rule Implementation

The GATT is based on a provisional treaty with a complex web of side codes and international agreements and provisions. It is extremely difficult to change the rules because the decision-making process in the GATT is based on consensus. Moreover, the implementation of GATT rules is impeded by loopholes, forum shopping, and the exercise of political power.

These shortcomings and weaknesses of the GATT were products of the trade policies of major countries, notably the United States and the EC. The change in the trade policy of the United States as the creator of the system affected the function and role of the GATT significantly.

Many articles of the GATT have their origin in U.S. trade law. In contrast, Japan was a passive norm taker, but her passive reaction to U.S. trade policy led to the weakening of the GATT system.

3. GATT and Japan's Trade Policy

The main laws relevant to trade policy are the Law on Foreign Exchange and Foreign Trade Control, coupled with the Government Ordinance on Export and Import Control, the Law on Export and Import Transactions, and the Customs Tariff Law. The Ministry of International Trade and Industry (MITI) implements administrative guidance based on these laws, ordinances, and other laws governing regulated industries. The first law listed above authorizes the minister of MITI to introduce an import quota system and an export approval system, while the second law acknowledges the formation of export and import cartels that are exempt from the Antimonopoly Law. The third law prescribes the conditions for the use of antidumping and countervailing duties.

When Japan was permitted to enter the GATT in 1955, fourteen countries invoked article 35 (nonapplication of GATT obligations) against Japan. At first Britain attempted to apply discretionary and selective safeguards against Japan as an alternative to article 35. But for Japan both article 35 and discretionary and selective safeguards implied severe restrictions on its competitive textile exports. Britain failed to apply selective safeguards against Japan because of the difficulty in amending the GATT articles. In 1956 Japan accommodated the U.S. request for voluntary export restraint on textiles. But the United States insisted on concluding an agreement at the administrative level in 1957. This agreement was extended at the GATT under the U.S. initiative to the MFA in 1961.

In 1963 Japan became subject to article 11, which prohibits the use of a tariff for balance-of-payment reasons. During the course of the 1960s and 1970s Japan promoted liberalization of trade and investment, resulting in a lower average tariff rate than those of other industrialized countries after the Tokyo Round. At the same time, Japan accommodated the U.S. request for voluntary restraint of exports of various products. Japan acted as a passive norm taker, regardless of the origin or legitimacy of the international norms.

In accommodating U.S. requests, administrative guidance was utilized on the basis of the Law on Export and Import Transactions and the Ordinance on Export Control. The MITI issued directives to create the export cartel on televisions (1963–73) and color televisions (1977–79) on the basis of the Law on Export and Import Transactions. Without these directives, the export cartel would have violated the Antitrust Law of the United States. Actually, the agreement between the U.S. government and Japan's Steel Export Association on export restraint of steel (1969–71) was brought to court because of the violation of the Antitrust Law by the U.S. Consumers' Union. In the case of automobiles (1981–90), the MITI simply issued a directive allocating export quotas to the companies concerned and monitored their adherence on the basis of the Foreign Exchange Control Law.

In Japan it is rare that private enterprises initiate petitions against the trade policy measures of the government. But this did occur with respect to the U.S.–Japan agreement on synthetic fiber and wool products in 1970. The agreement was the outcome of a political bargain involving export restraints and the reversion of Okinawa to Japan. The Japanese government implemented a voluntary quantitative export restraint on synthetic fiber and wool products based on the Ordinance of Export Control. But the Japanese Textile Industry Federation presented the case to a court and argued that the application of the ordinance violates article 11 of GATT (prohibition of quantitative restraint of imports and exports) and article 20 of the constitution (freedom of occupation and trade). The judgment was not delivered because the federation withdrew the lawsuit due to the renegotiation on textile at GATT in 1974. Yet this case casts doubt about the consistency of administrative discretionary measure with the GATT and the Constitution. This case pointed to the need of more rule-based trade policy equipped with more clarity of principles and transparency in the decision-making process. It also raised the issue of consistency of domestic laws and ordinances with the GATT rules.

Another case was the petition by the necktie producers on the import restriction based on the Law of Silk Yarn Price Stabilization. The necktie producers insisted that the silk yarn protection violates freedom of occupation and trade called for in the constitution. The suit was rejected by the court, which pointed as recourse to the safeguards clause (GATT article 19). But the legal procedure to apply the safeguards clause is not clearly stated in domestic laws. Actually, the safeguards provisions of the Foreign Exchange Control Law cannot be employed by private parties, although it is possible to exert political influence on the government's decision. It is within the discretion of the government (Matsushita 1990).

Judging from past history, Japan's trade policy was largely a reaction against the restrictive measures of its trading partners and their governments' request to liberalize access to its market.[3] Japan has scarcely taken initiative to strengthen the liberal world trading system. It is unfortunate that Japan is seen as a proponent of managed trade despite the fact that it was obliged by foreign countries to adopt "voluntary" export restraint from the beginning of its membership in GATT. Moreover, Japan is regarded by foreign observers as a successful case of adopting strategic policy; Tyson and Zysman (1989) named this policy the "moving band of protectionism" (liberalizing trade only after over-investment in a protected domestic market accompanied by concentrated exports abroad), although the policy simply moved toward trade liberalization after catching up with the level of Western technology, albeit maybe too slowly and gradually. This is not an unusual historical pattern in economic development.

It may be noted that Japan lacks judicial instruments by which to implement "strategic policy" in the sense of affecting a partner's behavior by influencing the partner's expectation. Aside from the antidumping and countervailing duties provisions, Japanese trade laws do not allow private businesses to initiate petitions. The detailed procedures on antidumping duties and countervailing duties were given only recently, in 1986; thus far only three cases have been brought forward for petition (cotton threads from Korea and Brazil and ferrosilicon from Brazil). This lack of judicial instruments suggests that the GATT should be more important in solving trade disputes for Japan than for the United States. Yet Japan has remained largely a passive participant in GATT negotiations. The initiative to revitalize the GATT stemmed from the United States, which has become more and more "strategic" in implementing trade policy.

The U.S. Move toward Strategic Trade Policy

In contrast to Japan's trade policy, U.S. trade policy is much more judicialized and subject to constitutional constraints. There is an unresolved ambiguity in U.S. constitutional law with respect to the division of power between the executive branch and Congress with regard to policy-making in international trade matters. The Reciprocal Trade Agreement Act of 1934 for the first time conferred upon the president broad advance authority to negotiate and conclude reciprocal trade agreements. Under this condition, the president accepted GATT. This trade authority was periodically renewed, allowing the United States to negotiate tariff reductions through the GATT. However, the GATT has never been consented to by Congress as a treaty obligation; it was regarded as an "executive agreement" superseded by domestic law until 1974.

The tension between Congress and the executive branch increased during the 1960s. The Trade Act of 1974 imposed constraints on executive discretion, while delegating to the president advance authority to negotiate nontariff barriers in the Tokyo Round and recognizing GATT as a binding international treaty through the authorization of appropriations for financial contributions to GATT. The Congress imposed constraints on presidential discretion in an attempt to ensure that the United States would not extend the benefits of trade barrier reduction to the industrial countries that refused to reciprocate adequately in the Tokyo Round negotiation. Section 301 was added to the trade law as a strong weapon against the free-rider problem inherent in the unconditional MFN of the GATT. Further, Congress judicialized existing import relief measures, including safeguards, antidumping, and countervailing duties, thereby empowering private parties to initiate petitions against foreign industry. Contingent protection flourished after the mid-1970s (table 4.4).

Ten years later, the 1984 act was the first broad legislation initiated by Congress, instead of the executive branch, since Smoot-Hawley. This authorized the president to negotiate a Free Trade Area Agreement with Israel and other countries. Subsequently, the Omnibus Trade and Competitiveness Act of 1988 strengthened retaliation against unfair trade practices in an effort to increase the international competitiveness of U.S. industries.

Section 301 was amended to enable the executive branch to adopt mandatory or discretionary retaliation when a partner country exercises unjustifiable, unreasonable, or discriminatory measures. "Unjustifiable" measures may include impediments to U.S. trade, such as anticompeti-

Table 4.4 Antidumping Duties and Countervailing Duties Initiated by the United States

	Antidumping Duties		Countervailing Duties	Safeguards
1970	22	7		
1971	39	13		
1972	27	13		
1973	10	3		
1974	10	6		
1975	27	9		
1976	15	4		
1977	44	12		
1978	44	3		
1979	17	4		
1980	14	1	7	2
1981	19	3	75	6
1982	38	5	35	4
1983	44	6	22	2
1984	61	3	60	6
1985	65	6	43	3
1986	43	9	11	5
1987	33	10	13	
1988	25	5	9	

Source: GATT-AD and CVD Committees.

tive business practices export targeting. "Super-301" (section 1302) prescribes the obligations of the USTR to present the Annual National Trade Estimate to Congress and to specify the priority unfair trade practices and priority countries within thirty days of the presentation of the estimate. It enabled unilateral determination of reciprocal fairness under the discretion of the executive branch. In 1989 Japan, Brazil, and India were specified as priority countries. In the case of Japan, unfair trade practices were cited for supercomputers, satellites, and lumber. In 1990 this provision expired in view of the progress made toward market access.

The "Structural Impediments Initiatives" dialogue between the United States and Japan was also begun in order to avoid escalation of retaliation based on section 301 and section 337 (protection of intellectual property). The Bush administration faced two tasks: the need to bring about the success of the Uruguay Round and the need to contain the protectionism of Congress. Priority was given to removing barriers to market access and correcting bilateral trade imbalances.[4]

Disappointment with the 1982 GATT Ministerial Meeting added momentum to the move toward bilateralism. The drift toward bilateralism may be viewed as a presidential counterattack against the more drastic protectionism of Congress. The United States embarked on the formation of a free trade area with the intention of further extending it to Central and Latin America. Ambassador William Brock of the Reagan administration described the move as a Super-GATT because it aimed to prompt trade liberalization by including a wider range of issues. However, from the viewpoint of foreign observers, trade policy under the 1988 act seems to imply a return to the bilateralism and aggressive reciprocity based on threats of retaliation, instead of promises, that had characterized U.S. trade policy before 1922. From a game-theory viewpoint, the current U.S. trade policy can be described as a policy based on a "tit-for-tat" strategy.

Although admitting the merits of strategic trade policy based on a tit-for-tat strategy, such as simplicity and uniqueness, Dixit (1987) argued that U.S. trade policy lacked clarity as to the conditions of retaliation and the certainty of retaliation (provocability), while it satisfied the requirements of niceness (not being the first to defect) and forgiveness. He concluded that a trade policy based on strategic moves, notably threats, will not work well.

Japan's trade policy also apparently satisfied the forgiveness requirement, but lacked clarity and provocability. Moreover, Japan missed the opportunity to be nice by accommodating U.S. requests for export restraint. Japan's trade policy was broadly reactive instead of strategic, although its export-oriented industrial policy may have created the impression that Japan pursued a "strategic" policy.

Importance of the Uruguay Round

In view of the defects of the GATT, the United States took the initiative to embark on a new round of trade negotiations in 1982. The United States focused on agricultural trade, and new areas such as trade in services, trade-related investment measures, and intellectual property rights; the excessive surplus of agricultural products on the world market became obvious in the 1980s, while agricultural subsidies rose enormously ($200 billion a year, according to the OECD estimate). The United States found that its comparative advantage in trade in services was not being reflected in its market position overseas. Additionally, the United States hoped to keep the European countries from excessively inward-looking regionalism ("Fortress Europe").

Although there appeared to be significant progress on a number of subjects such as tariffs, nontariffs, natural resource products, tropical products, and rules of product origin, the negotiations deadlocked on the issue of agricultural trade. The issues addressed in the Uruguay Round may be summarized by the following nine areas.

1. Regarding agricultural products, the United States initially proposed to convert quantitative trade barriers to tariffs and to aim at reducing both tariff and export subsidies to the agricultural sector to zero in ten years. A revised proposal sought a target tariff reduction of 75 percent on domestic subsidies and 90 percent on export subsidies. The EC Commission made a counterproposal to reduce agricultural protection 30 percent over ten years starting in 1986, based on the aggregate measurement support (AMS).[5] Japan insisted on excluding rice and some dairy products from tariffication because of the food security. In September 1990 Japan accepted a 30 percent reduction in domestic protection. However, the U.S. and EC positions could not be compromised in the December 1990 ministerial conference, and this difference remains the key block to the conclusion of the Uruguay Round.

2. Regarding services, it was agreed upon to establish the right of national treatment, the transparency of barriers, and progressive liberalization of trade in services. There remains the issue as to whether we should include in the negotiation services involving the movement of capital and labor, notably unskilled migrant labor. In addition, the EC argues for effective market access based on reciprocity and discriminatory treatment against countries that do not comply with reciprocity. The United States seems to accept the EC proposal, while Japan objects to the idea of discrimination on the ground of the principle of reciprocity.

3. Regarding trade-related investment measures (TRIMs), the trade-off between the need for development and the private incentive to invest is not resolved. Developing countries argue that local content and export performance requirements serve to promote development and thus are

justified by GATT article 17c. Yet it is necessary to exclude new barriers and establish the red-light prohibitions against offensive performance requirements for export, trade balancing, employment, local manufacturing, and local content as well as foreign exchange restrictions by host countries.

4. Regarding trade-related intellectual property rights (TRIPs), it is necessary to create consensus on a minimum standard of protection of property rights (copyright, patent, trademark, design, trade secrecy). Developing countries argue that the issue must be handled by the World Intellectual Property Organization (WIPO) aside from the prohibition against pirated and counterfeit goods. But the WIPO lacks an effective enforcement mechanism. In addition, there exists a basic difficulty in striking a balance between the provision of incentive for knowledge creation (innovation) and the use of the knowledge (technology transfer). Among developed countries there are also different views on the patent system (a first-to-invent or a first-to-file method) and on the extension of copyright to neighboring rights, given the divergent prescriptions of domestic laws on patents.

5. Regarding safeguards, opinion is divided as to whether there could be selective activation of safeguards. Selective application of safeguards not only violates the nondiscrimination principle but also creates vested interests in the countries not being targeted, as the MFA has demonstrated.

The U.S.–Canada Free Trade Area Agreement allowed selectivity in dispute settlements on safeguard measures: the dispute settlement mechanism is regarded as one of the major accomplishments in the adjudication of contingent measures. The agreement exempted each country from others' global safeguard restrictions when the partners do not form an important part of the injury. This violates article 24 (free-trade area), which requires removal of all safeguard measures. It also negates the full application of the MFN of article 19 (safeguard measures). Thus, at the Uruguay Round the United States moved from support of nonselectivity to support of limited selectivity subject to multilateral surveillance and degressivity.

It is easy to see why the EC pushes strongly to adopt the selective approach; the formation and extension of regional groupings can be strengthened through discriminatory application of safeguards to the third-person countries. The U.S. commitment to the bilateral free-trade agreement with Canada anticipated the U.S. move toward selectivity. Japan stands firm against application of selective safeguards because of the bitter experience of having article 35 invoked against it when it entered the GATT. Yet it may be noted that Japan accommodated the request by the United States and the EC on the VERs, which are the functional equivalents of selective safeguards originating from the need for structural adaptation. There is a trade-off between the abolition of gray area measures and the adoption of selective application of safeguards under clearly stated conditions and time limits.

6. Regarding textiles and clothing, it was agreed at Montreal in December 1988 to phase out the restrictions under the MFA, since they were deemed GATT-incompatible. There appeared two proposals: the global quotas method (advocated by the United States) or gradual dismantling of all MFA restrictions based on the MFA growth solution (by raising the import ceiling of the MFA) in ten years (advocated by the developing countries and Japan).

7. Regarding subsidies and countervailing duties, it was agreed to prohibit export-promoting subsidies while specifying the conditions for triggering countervailing duties and limiting them to five years' duration. The United States was reluctant to broaden the green-light subsidies, while the EC is more tolerant toward subsidies. Subsidies for regional development, precompetitive R&D, environmental protection, and employment adjustment were included in the green-light subsidies. But there remains the issue of the extent to which subsidies to precompetitive R&D are to be permitted. In addition, Japan insists that subsidies for structural adjustment in declining industries such as ship building and coal mining be permitted.

8. The United States proposed to allow for retaliation against "repeat dumping" while the EC suggested adoption of the rule against "screwdriver plants" and the "export of parts" that are designed to circumvent antidumping duties. Japan objects strongly to retaliation against repeat dumping. One complication is interrelations of these suggested measures with the TRIMs. To avoid antidumping, a company must obey the local content requirement, but this may contradict the object of the TRIMs.

9. Regarding dispute settlement, the EC and Japan propose to prohibit unilateral retaliation: the U.S. practice, based on section 301, was found to be incompatible with GATT rules. While it seems difficult to strengthen the enforcement mechanism of GATT panel decisions,

contracting parties are likely to agree not to block the establishment of panels, the adoption of panel reports, or compliance with panel decisions. The introduction of an appellate tribunal of legal experts may be approved.

Japan seems to have been successful in supporting its position on safeguards, the MFA, subsidies, and countervailing duties. However, Japan cannot escape blame with respect to the failure to agree on agricultural trade, although this failure stemmed from a dispute between the United States and the EC. In order to save the GATT negotiation, it is of utmost importance for Japan to join with the United States to persuade the EC regarding agricultural trade liberalization. Japan should make concessions on agricultural products; the partial liberalization of rice imports should be implemented with the ceiling of 2 percent (0.2 million tons), or 5 percent of domestic production, despite the resolution against liberalization of rice imports at the Diet. It is also desirable to impose some constraints on export subsidies for agricultural products. The United States may make a concession in delaying the time allowed for tariffication and in the size of tariff reduction. In new areas such as services, including the TRIPs and the TRIMs, progress may occur despite resistance by developing countries. With respect to unfair trade practices and safeguards, we need more far-reaching solutions, as discussed below, if the core problem lies in the rebalance of the burden of adjustment costs among countries with different economic structure. Given the disharmony and widespread disappointment among participants in the Uruguay Round talks, we may need to restructure the world trading system more fundamentally.

4. New World Trade System after the Uruguay Round

Depending on the degree of success of the Uruguay Round, there are four alternative scenarios for the formation of a new world trading system in the 1990s.

The first scenario would be the formation of three regional groupings. If the Uruguay Round runs aground, there will be an increased inclination toward the formation of regional groupings. But the formation of regional groupings may reduce world welfare due to discrimination among the three areas. Krugman (1989) argues convincingly that the three groupings scenario would be the worst, given monopolistic competition and the optimal tariff available to each region; the larger size of a regional grouping implies a larger trade-creation effect. Nevertheless, this kind of grouping is accompanied by an even larger trade diversion and a higher optimal tariff rate.

In the second scenario, a code approach to strengthening the GATT system could be taken. The Atlantic Council of the United States (1975) once proposed a "GATT plus" based on codes in the form of a package deal. This approach was also developed by Hufbauer and Schott (1985). Several economists advocate the usefulness of a code approach—notably on subsidies, safeguards, and services—in securing a balance between nondiscrimination and the penalties of free riding (Baldwin and Richardson 1987), while others regard the code approach as a serious derogation from GATT norms.

The code approach can promote liberalization of trade and investment in the Pacific area, which consists of countries at different development stages (Iwata 1988). This approach is essentially based on plurilateralism: the most-favored-nations clause is applied only to those who want to participate in the liberalization process. Thus it replaces unconditional MFN by conditional MFN, with the aim of eliminating free riding.

The third scenario for the creation of a new world trading system would involve establishment of an OECD free trade and investment area. A code approach centering on the conditional MFN concept was advanced in a proposal to establish on OECD free trade and investment area by G. Hufbauer (1989). He anticipates limited success for the Uruguay Round and argues for an enlarged free-trade and investment area. An OECD-FTIA is attractive in two respects. First, it may help discourage the EC from adopting an excessively inward-looking policy. Second, it would seem relatively easy to realize an OECD-FTIA in view of the accomplishment of trade and investment liberalization by the OECD member countries. It is encouraging that in May 1990 the OECD member countries reached agreement on liberalization of direct investment based on national treatment with respect to taxation, subsidies, and government procurement. This agreement precludes new requirements on local content and other regulations.

One of the major defects of this proposal is the discriminatory effect it could have on developing countries. Hufbauer contends that such discriminatory effects may be minor, due to higher growth in the area, easy entry to the area, and diminished gray area measures. However, it seems likely that the tension between the South and the North may be heightened, unless institutional arrangements are made regarding access to a dispute-settlement mechanism within the OECD-FTIA by developing countries. Another problem is duplication at the level of international organizations. Both the GATT and the OECD would virtually become legal constitutions for trade policy. In addition, even more than the GATT Secretariat, the OECD lacks experts on law and dispute settlement.

In view of the move toward regionalism by the EC and the United States and the thus-far unsuccessful outcome of the Uruguay Round talks, Malaysia's Prime Minister Mahathir bin Mohamed proposed the East Asian Economic Group, excluding Australia, the United States, and Canada. The United States criticized the proposal while Japan has not expressed any official view. Yet Japan's basic thrust of policy lies in open regionalism of the Pacific area, including the United States and Canada; Japan has already taken the initiative to develop the Pacific Economic Cooperation Conference (PECC) and the Asia-Pacific Economic Cooperation (APEC) together with Australia and Singapore. These institutions are oriented toward open regionalism and can be characterized by informality and flexibility; nondiscrimination in action and nonexclusivity of international relations constitute the core principles of open regionalism. Increasing business ties between U.S. and Japanese multinationals created by direct foreign investment and the concomitant outward processing of high-tech industries has contributed to the production and exports of Asian countries, although the share of foreign capital in total capital stock is smaller than for Latin American countries. Japan is expected to play a key role in absorbing Asian exports of manufactured products and in providing capital, management, and technology to Asian countries. Regardless of the success or failure of the Uruguay Round talks, open regionalism in the Pacific area will continue to evolve in the forthcoming decade. The close business interdependence among the United States, Japan, and the Asian countries seems to negate the formation of an Asian bloc in the near future.

The fourth and final possible scenario would entail the establishment of a multilateral trade organization. Jackson (1990) proposed to restructure the world trading system by legally consolidating the GATT to establish the World Trade Organization (WTO). This proposal was endorsed by Italy and then Canada, and it received basic accord at the Quadrangular Meeting of Trade Ministers in May 1990. The EC preferred to name it the "Multilateral Trade Organization" (MTO), putting emphasis on the importance of multilateralism, as opposed to unilateralism or bilateralism, in dispute settlements. At the G-7 Summit in July 1990 it was agreed that the issue of the MTO should be discussed after the Uruguay Round. The Functioning of the GATT Group (FOG) has taken up the issue as an agenda item.

The main purpose of the MTO is to restore the GATT as an international organization comparable to the IMF and the IBRD. This idea was originally envisaged in the Havana Charter for the International Trade Organization (ITO) and was revived in 1955 as the Organization for Trade Cooperation (OTC). It aims at (1) achieving legal integrity for the GATT articles and various codes and other arrangements; (2) improving dispute settlement procedures to preclude forum shopping; and (3) providing an interface mechanism for new participating nonmarket economies.

The MTO is reminiscent of the International Trade Organization with a universal membership principle, which allows the fullest feasible participation of all countries. Universal membership corresponds to the notion of collective security under the aegis of the United Nations. It may be recalled that the UN charter regards the GATT as a specialized agency under the UN system. The universality principle has gained its importance in constructing a new world order. The transition of Communist countries to a market-oriented system augments the need for the GATT as an interface mechanism to facilitate trade among nations with different economic systems.

U.S. President Truman withdrew ratification of the ITO in view of strong congressional resistance in December 1950. If the MTO can really function as a super international organization to settle disputes and to effectively enforce panel decisions in member countries, this is an ideal solution for solving trade problems. Bilateral and regional approaches to removing differences of economic structure among different countries will be replaced and integrated by the MTO; dispute settlement will be monitored multilaterally so that the side effects inherent in a bilateral or plurilateral approach to free trade may be minimized.

It is encouraging that major countries tend to rely more on recourse to panel decisions in solving trade disputes; it is interesting to note that for the first time the United States changed domestic law to make it compatible with the GATT in 1981, in response to the complaint by the EC on the Domestic International Corporation (DISC). Further, in 1988 Japan implemented liberalization of ten agricultural products based on the decision of a panel. At the same time, Japan for the first time initiated a GATT panel based on article 23 and Antidumping Code 15. The panel was against the application of an antidumping duty by the EC on parts imported from Japan. The EC also started to give more attention to GATT panel decisions. It seems promising to create norms and to consolidate a legal constitution by strengthening the dispute-settlement mechanism on a multilateral basis.

Economic Aspects of Restructuring the GATT

Aside from the legal aspects, we should not dismiss the economic or game-theoretical aspects of restructuring the world trading system. From the standpoint of economists committed to global liberalism, trade policy issues must be handled on the basis of economic principles of efficiency and income distribution. The policy recommendations by such economists are straightforward:

1. Adopt a trade policy of unilateral liberalization and adhere to the nondiscrimination norm and the unconditional MFN procedure; in a competitive market structure, unilateral liberalization of trade improves the welfare of the country, even though trading countries maintain protection.
2. Provide structural adjustment assistance through international institutions to industries suffering from dynamic changes in trade structure; a structural adjustment fund at the GATT may be funded by collecting subsidies and tariff revenues from all the countries. This fund could provide internationally monitored subsidies and serve to solve the problem of structural adaptation and income distribution. Moreover, it may be desirable to provide subsidies to precompetitive R&D to avoid excessive R&D rivalry among competing nations, thereby countering the move toward technonationalism.
3. Apply a standardized antimonopoly law to all countries to inhibit monopolistic gain and to protect consumers' interests. This will di-

minish the merits of adopting strategic trade policy in order to snatch monopolistic rent and will serve to prevent the tendency toward an oligopolistic market structure.

4. Harmonize domestic regulations, law, and taxation systems to secure market opportunities for all.

For the economists who firmly believe that a liberal economic order emerges spontaneously from rational behavior by individuals, the free-trade regime is supported by the rational self-interest of individuals. The commitment to global liberalism by nations is inherently consistent with individualism. Those who commit unilaterally to free trade may be described as "everyday Kantinesians" seeking perpetual world peace.

But game theorists would contend that the problem of an international economic order arises from a discrepancy between individual rationality and a nation's rationality. Even in a perfectly competitive market, the government is lured to raise tariffs to an optimal level if that country can affect the price in the world market. By raising tariffs that way the country enjoys an additional terms-of-trade gain (optimal tariff). Under imperfect competition, the opportunity to snatch monopolistic rent by adopting strategic trade and industrial policies is widened.

Every country pursues its own strategic trade policy, explicitly or implicitly. What is required are rules for implementing strategies. Certain strategies must be eliminated from the range of choices or must be constrained by rules if we want to preserve a cooperative solution.[6] When the GATT was established, it implied a peace treaty ending the trade war of the 1930s. This peace treaty can be regarded as a cooperative solution that brings about a Pareto improvement in the world economy trapped in a Prisoner's Dilemma situation.

Cooperation by Uncooperative Behavior

Within a framework of repeated games based on rational behavior of the players with an infinite time horizon, it can be shown that a cooperative solution can be supported by uncooperative strategic behavior, given sufficient patience or far-sightedness of the players. But the cooperative solution is not necessarily stable; it is susceptible to defect and disturbance. Moreover, if the players are very patient (which implies that the discount rate of future benefit is close to zero), then any rational payoff can be supported as an equilibrium outcome; there exist too many equilibriums (this is known as the "Folk Theorem") (Friedman 1986).

On the basis of the evolutionary approach, Axelrod (1986) argues that cooperation emerges from normative behavior by individuals employing a tit-for-tat strategy. A player's strategy is normative in the sense that it can affect the other party's expectation in the direction the player desires. Recent U.S. trade policy putting emphasis on reciprocity, the conditional MFN, and retaliation accords well with the tit-for-tat strategy. But the conditional MFN violates the norm of nondiscrimination, while unilateral judgment on unfairness and bilateralism of retaliation against unfair countries is not compatible with the multilateralism and due process of GATT.[7] The threats implicit in the strategy are not necessarily creditable because gain from unilateral free trade is presumably much larger than loss from trade war; this strategy lacks subgame perfection. In addition, the tit-for-tat strategy does not secure a cooperative solution, although it intends to induce cooperation; if the partner defects once, then endless defection (trade war) follows.

Stabilizing a Cooperative Solution

Binding agreements or norms can work to sustain and stabilize a cooperative regime. Axelrod (1986) proposes to apply metanorms to strengthen the effectiveness of norms. "Metanorm" refers to punishment not only against violators but also against anyone who refuses to punish the defector. It presupposes a strict enforcement mechanism that may contradict individual liberalism. The alternative to the establishment of metanorms is law.

Another way to stabilize a cooperative solution is to prohibit the use of the strategy of "always noncooperate" or "always defect" and to provide incentives for adopting the strategy of "always cooperate." Yet unilateral liberalism could provide incentives for other countries to act as free riders or foot draggers. This holds true with respect to the unconditional MFN. It must be remembered that excessive provision of public goods could destroy the liberal order.

In order to eliminate adoption of the "always defect" strategy, it seems necessary to increase the cost of defection to a prohibitive level. The public choice theorists would propose changing the voting rule: passage of legislation on trade restriction measures against free trade

Table 4.5 Payoff Matrix of the "Prisoner's Dilemma" and the "Stag Hunt"

(A) Prisoner's Dilemma	Cooperation	Noncooperation
Cooperation	5/5	− 3/8
Noncooperation	8/ − 3	0/0

(B) Stag Hunt	Cooperation	Noncooperation
Cooperation	8/8	− 6/5
Noncooperation	5/ − 6	− 3/ − 3

should require a two-thirds majority both at the national and the international level (GATT). This may help eliminate the choice of the "always defect" strategy.[8]

As an alternative to a voting rule, the proposal to raise the economic cost of protection by establishing rules to levy an international tax on protection and trade-distorting measures should be considered. Combined with international subsidies for structural adaptations, the international tax would work to transform the payoff matrix of countries from the Prisoner's Dilemma into the Stag Hunt, where the cooperative gain is larger than the cheating gain; that is, the gain of hunting stag cooperatively is larger than that of uncooperative rabbit hunting (J. J. Rousseau). Table 4.5 presents the payoff matrix of the Stag Hunt in comparison with the Prisoner's Dilemma. The loss is larger if the two players adopt the "always defect" strategy. The gain of reneging is smaller due to the tax, while subsidies are provided for a cooperative strategy. As a result, the international tax and subsidy system strengthens the cooperative regime. It could also serve to reinforce the enforcement and compensation mechanisms (GATT article 23 on nullification and impairment).

5. Conclusion and Policy Proposal

From the preceding analyses we can draw several policy proposals for restructuring the world trading system and for the trade policy required of Japan.

  1. To maintain a free trade system, the Uruguay Round must be

successful. Japan should act positively to ensure the success of the negotiation by allowing the liberalization of agricultural products, including
rice: the United States must refrain from implementing a unilateral
trade policy. The nondiscrimination principle must be preserved for
safeguards, while the MFA restrictions must be dismantled within ten
years based on the MFA growth approach. It is adequate to agree on
codes on trade in services, the TRIMs and the TRIPs; they provide
the basic framework on the right of establishment, national treatment,
transparency, nondiscrimination, and the minimum standard of protection of intellectual property.

2. Japan should support and promote the legal restructuring of the
GATT (MTO) to strengthen the multilateral dispute settlement and
enforcement mechanisms.

3. This legal restructuring can be supplemented by the introduction
of an international tax and subsidy system into the GATT. First, the
structural adjustment fund must be created at the GATT to rebalance
the costs of adjustment arising from dynamic change in comparative
advantage. This may diminish the need to rely on contingent protection,
gray area measures, and, thus, managed trade. Further, if the fund
provides subsidies to precompetitive R&D as an international public
good, it would serve to mitigate R&D rivalry and prevent technonationalism from being dominant. Japan should take the lead in providing the
basic R&D to the world economy to ward off the criticism by trading
partners of having a selfish "strategic policy." Second, it is necessary
to eliminate protectionism (the "always protect" strategy) by levying
international taxes on protection.

4. Japan should seek to harmonize domestic regulations, administrative procedures, and law with international standards. Notably, stan-
dardization of antimonopoly law across borders is important in view of
the trend toward an oligopolistic structure of world trade and abuse of
strategic trade policy. The consistent and strengthened competition policy may diminish the incentive to adopt strategic policy aimed at gaining
monopolistic rent. Minilateralism and plurilateralism could play certain
roles in achieving this goal. But the result of liberalization of trade
arising from harmonization must be easily accessible to the third-person
countries. Multilateral trade negotiation should consciously aim at reap-
ing the results of minilateral or plurilateral approaches to free trade.

5. It is desirable to transform the SII dialogue into a more permanent

institution to deal with trade disputes. The SII went beyond the scope of usual trade negotiations and focused on issues not covered at the Uruguay Round or the bilateral negotiation based on Super-301. The SII can be interpreted as an attempt to prepare the next stage for a single-market or "borderless" economy by promoting the harmonization of administrative procedures, institutions, regulations, business practices, and competition policy. The SII will also work to reduce nontariff barriers and the need to use contingent protection.[9] At some stage this mechanism must be transferred to the newly created MTO.

6. Any move toward closed regionalism in the Asia-Pacific area should be avoided regardless of the success or failure of the Uruguay Round talks. Japan should continue to take the initiative in promoting free trade and investment in the Pacific in close collaboration with the United States; Japan should act as an absorber of manufactured products and a provider of capital and technology in this area.

Notes

1. For a more detailed description of the three regional groupings, see Iwata (1990).
2. Lincoln finds all methods of adjustment of overall trade imbalance unsatisfactory and employs only an unadjusted intraindustry index. But international comparison of indices seems to require some form of adjustment, if a country registers a large trade imbalance.
3. Voluntary export restraints were implemented either at the request of the U.S. government or by unilateral action. On the issue of relations between the constitution and the ordinance in Japan with respect to trade policy, see Matsushita (1988).
4. The United States' first move toward bilateralism was the U.S.–Canada Automotive Products Agreement in 1965, wherein the two countries obtained a waiver from their MFN obligations at the GATT. In the 1980s the new wave surged with the Caribbean Initiative (1983), which was followed by the Free Trade Area Agreement with Israel (1985), Mexico (1987), and Canada (1988). Bilateral negotiations with Japan in the Market-Oriented-Sector-Selective (MOSS) in the earlier part of the 1980s brought about modest success. They were superseded by the Structural Impediments Initiatives (SII) after 1989.
5. The aggregate measurement support is the index of protection in terms of market access, domestic price support, and export subsidies: the AMS excludes nontrade distorting measures from the public subsidy equivalent (PSE).
6. Japan's industrial policy is often cited as a successful case. But the economic

basis for the industrial policy is shaky. Suzumura and Okuno (1987) conclude that the role of industrial policy can be found only in the case of coordination failure, information acquisition, and information sharing under incomplete information. These roles have little relationship to strategic trade policy aimed at obtaining monopolistic rent and protecting the domestic market.

7. U.S. trade policy seems to be in a halfway house with respect to the conditional MFN, which was abandoned in 1922 under the Harding administration. Bilateral reciprocal negotiation was initiated with the Cobden-Chevalier Treaty in 1860. This approach entailed negotiating chaos with costly and uneasy renegotiations with prior signees necessitated every time new bilateral agreement was reached. The fact that the cost can be rendered more tolerable by multilateralism was one of the factors that moved U.S. trade policy toward multilateralism.

8. Grubel (1989) proposes to adopt the change in voting procedure. Alternatively, it may be possible to declare in the constitution that trade restrictions are inconsistent with an individual's freedom of occupation and trade. It may be recalled that the invocation of article 35 requires a two-thirds majority at the GATT.

9. The Structural Impediments Initiative was the first attempt to make proposals on fiscal policy coordination. Fiscal policy coordination is regarded as one of the most difficult areas, even for EC countries. The initial U.S. request on expansion of public investment was excessive; the request to increase the public investment–GNP ratio by 3–4 percentage points in the forthcoming decade may reduce the current account surplus to zero or even negative, given the constant domestic-savings ratio and private-investment ratio. Japan would cease to be a capital exporter since its financial power would be eroded.

References

Atlantic Council of the United States (1975). *GATT Plus: A Proposal for Trade Reform.* Washington, D.C.

Axelrod, R. (1981). "The Emergence of Cooperation among Egoists." *American Political Science Review* 75, no. 2 (June).

——— (1986). "An Evolutionary Approach to Norms." *American Political Science Review* 80, no. 4 (December).

Baldwin, R. E. (1988). *Trade Policy in a Changing World.* Harvester-Wheatsheaf.

Baldwin, R. E., and J. D. Richardson (1987). "Recent U.S. Trade Policy and Its Global Implications." In C. I. Bradford, Jr., and W. H. Branson, eds., *Trade and Structural Change in Pacific Asia.* University of Chicago Press.

Dixit, A. (1987). "How Should the United States Respond to Other Countries' Trade Policies?" In R. M. Stern, ed., *U.S. Trade Policies in a Changing World Economy.* MIT Press.

Dogauchi, M. (1989). "International Trade in Services from the Japanese Viewpoint." *Georgia Journal of International and Comparative Law* 19, no. 2.

Dornbusch, R. (1990). "Policy Options for Freer Trade: The Case for Bilateralism." In R. Z. Lawrence and C. L. Schulz, eds., *An American Strategy in the 1990s*. Brookings Institution.

Friedman, J. W. (1986). *Game Theory with Application to Economics*. Oxford University Press.

Grubel, H. (1989). "Does the World Need a GATT for Services?" In Hans-Jurgen Vorerau, ed., *New Institutional Arrangements for the World Economy*. Springer-Verlag.

Hufbauer, G. C. (1989). Background Paper to "The Free Trade Debate" (*Reports of the Twentieth-Century Fund Task Force on the Future of American Trade Policy*). New York: Priority Press Publications.

Hufbauer, G. C., and J. J. Schott (1985). "Trading for Growth: The Next Round of Trade Negotiations." *Policy Analyses in International Economics,* no. 11, Institute for International Economics.

Iwata, K. (1988). "U.S.–Japan Economic Relations: A Japanese Perspective." Working Paper no. 7, Department of Social and International Relations, University of Tokyo, September.

——— (1989). "Changes of Economic and Trade Structure in the Pacific-Basin Area." Paper presented for the Asia-Pacific Conference organized by the FAIR, June.

——— (1990). "Economic Perspective in the 1990s." Paper presented at the U.S.–Japan Business Conference at Osaka, July.

——— (1991). "Japan's Intraindustry Trade and Intrafirm Trade in the 1980s." Paper presented for the Second Asia-Pacific Conference organized by the FAIR, 9–10 May.

Jackson, J. (1989). *The World Trading System*. MIT Press.

——— (1990). *Restructuring the GATT System*. Royal Institute of International Affairs.

Kondo, T. (1989). "Is Normative Behavior Needed to Maintain Social Order?" Mimeo, July.

Krugman, P. (1989). "Is Bilateralism Bad?" NBER Working Paper, no. 2972, May.

Lawrence, R. Z. (1987). "Imports in Japan: Closed Markets or Minds?" Brookings Papers on Economic Activity, no. 2.

Lincoln, E. J. (1990). *Japan's Unequal Trade*. Brookings Institution.

Matsushita, M. (1988). *International Economic Law* (in Japanese). Yuhikaku.

——— (1990). "Comments on Antidumping Law Enforcement in Japan." In J. H. Jackson and E. A. Vermulst, eds., *Antidumping Law and Practice—A Comparative Study*. Harvester Wheatsheaf.

Patterson, G. (1987). "Comment on 'Multilateral and Bilateral Negotiating Approaches for the Conduct of U.S. Trade Policies' (John H. Jackson)." In R. M. Stern, ed., *U.S. Trade Policies in a Changing World Economy*. MIT Press.

Sazanami, Y., and H. Urata (1990). *Service Trade* (in Japanese). Toyo Keizai Shinposha.

Schott, J. J., ed. (1990). *Completing the Uruguay Round: A Result-Oriented Approach to the GATT Trade Negotiations.* Institute for International Economics.

Schott, J. J., and M. G. Smith, eds. (1988). *The Canada–United States Free Trade Agreement: The Global Impact.* Institute for International Economics and Institute for Research on Public Policy.

Stern, R. M. (1987). *U.S. Trade Policies in a Changing World Economy.* MIT Press.

Stern, R. M., P. H. Trezise, and J. Whalley (1987). *Perspectives on a U.S.–Canada Free Trade Agreement.* Brookings Institution.

Suzumura, K., and M. Okuno (1987). "Industrial Policy in Japan: Overview and Evaluation." In R. Sato and P. Wachtel, eds., *Trade Friction and Economic Policy.* Cambridge University Press.

Tyson, L. (1990). "Managed Trade: Making the Best of the Second Best." In R. Z. Lawrence and C. L. Schulz, eds., *An American Strategy in the 1990s.* Brookings Institution.

Tyson, L., and J. Zysman (1989). "Developmental Strategy and Production Innovation in Japan." In C. Johnson, L. Tyson, and J. Zysman, eds., *Politics and Productivity: The Real Story of Why Japan Works.* Ballinger.

5. Japan's Role in Economic Cooperation and Direct Foreign Investment

Makoto Sakurai

In the 1980s the position of developing countries with regard to global money flow was quite different from that of the 1960s and 1970s. In spite of the development and growth of the world economy, many developing countries found themselves facing problems such as huge debt burdens, serious deficits in their balance of payments, higher inflation, and so on. Especially in global money flow, developing countries as a whole had a negative net resources transfer in the 1980s.[1] And even now we can see a net resources transfer from developing to developed countries. Under this pattern of global money flow in the 1980s, Japan has appeared as a new and major capital-exporting economy.

Japan's economic cooperation has begun to sharply increase in terms of volume of funds since about the mid-1980s. It registered the highest growth, along with items related to national defense, in the fiscal expenditure of the budget. Currently, Japan has turned out to be the world's greatest donor of economic cooperation. Furthermore, in the latter half of the 1980s, accumulated debt problems of the third world, particularly in Latin American countries, have grown serious. This has induced Japan to actively extend financial cooperation to these countries as a part of its debt relief measures, in addition to providing Official Development Assistance (ODAs). Also, the historical wave of democratization that occurred in Eastern Europe in 1989 has posed an important question about the economic reconstruction to take place in the decade to follow. In this respect, the role that Japan will play in the area of economic and financial cooperation will be regarded as significant.

Japan actually implements economic and financial cooperation in the diversified forms of ODA, financial cooperation, technological cooperation, and direct foreign investment, among other things. Japan's part in the international community in the 1990s will become notable in the area of such contributions. However, in spite of the steep and substantial expansion in the volume of fund flows, the existing domestic system still resembles the one that came into being in the 1970s and lasted until the first half of the 1980s, reminding us of various tasks that need to be carried out and problems that need to be solved.

In the 1990s the potential financial needs from developing countries (heavily indebted developing countries in Latin America and developing countries in Asia) and Newly Democratizing Countries (NDCs) in East Europe will be great. However, the present situation of worldwide savings is not sufficient to satisfy potential worldwide financial needs.

Economic cooperation and financial cooperation will become one of the major cards in the international power game under the "post–Cold War" system in the 1990s.

Here I will attempt to look into Japan's current problems, paying particular attention to economic cooperation, and will also touch on newly emerging tasks facing Eastern Europe and Latin American countries. Finally, I will take up the issue of global economic cooperation and the tasks involved in this respect.

1. Japan's Transformation into a Capital Exporter and a Major Power in Economic Assistance

Japan's international balance of payments for calendar year 1989 was comprised of the current account balance of payments, registering $57 billion in surplus, and the long-term capital account balance of payments, indicating $87.9 billion in deficit. Thus, the country turned out to be the biggest capital-exporting country in the world. In terms of external net assets, the levels of $291.7 billion and $293.2 billion were reached for 1988 and 1989, respectively. In the end of 1989, the external net assets outstanding amounted to $1,771.0 billion, making Japan the greatest creditor in the international community.[2]

Economic cooperation embraces diverse contents, including the fostering of human resources and technological assistance among its priority items. But ODAs and the recycling of funds to developing countries play key roles among various forms of capital exports to developing countries. In terms of value, ODAs and recycling of funds are greater in comparison to other forms of economic cooperation. When one contemplates the tasks for Japan in the 1990s, when it will be a major capital exporter and donor of economic assistance, one sees that it is essential to put forms of capital exports in order.

For the purpose of continuous capital exports in the medium and long terms, maintaining the current account balance in surplus becomes a precondition. The current account surplus under the heading of domestic economy refers to the extent to which the level of national savings surpasses that of domestic investments. The current account surplus in the mid-1980s even outperformed the nominal rate of GNP, which was 4.5 percent. This ratio sharply declined in subsequent years to be about 1 percent at present. As mentioned earlier, Japanese capital exports registered the net value of $87.9 billion in 1989, exceeding by far the level of the current account surplus.

Financial resources of capital exports by economic units can be roughly divided into two categories. First, the public sector constitutes official development assistance and, second, the recycling of funds constitutes a form of public fund including export credit in deferred payment. On entering the second half of the 1980s, Japanese ODAs indicated a high growth of 6–8 percent. In particular, defense-related expenses and social welfare–related expenses each recorded the highest growth ever. In terms of value, ¥733.9 billion was represented by ODA in the FY 1989 budget. In the draft budget for FY 1990, the share of ODA indeed amounted to ¥784.5 billion, reaching the level of approximately $50–$60 billion (when converted on the basis of $1/¥150 exchange rate, this amounts to $52.3 billion). In addition to this program for ODA, there is a recycling of funds plan in the amount of $30 billion in the aggregate, which was launched in 1986. This plan to channel funds into developing countries and the ODA program overlap. Close to $10 billion is in the form of OOF (Other Official

Flows), and OOF and ODA in the aggregate amount of $10 billion or more per annum flows out of Japan to developing countries. In 1989, this program was extended to 1992, and the total amount was also raised to $65 billion.

Another source of funds is comprised of capital exports from the private sector, which include securities investment, private loans, and direct foreign investment. It is distinct from capital exports from the public sector, wherein allocation of financial resources is decided in accordance with policy measures. Apart from ODAs and the recycling of funds, which are independent of the market mechanism in their allocation, this source of funding from the private sector is allocated through a filter of the market mechanism, or profitability. Since this type of flow is characterized by the fact that it is based on the market mechanism, however, the allocation of funds may lean toward specified economies or regions. For example, in the case of securities investment, it is virtually limited to industrialized countries due to the fact that securities markets in many of the developing countries are not yet adequately developed for such a purpose. Private loans and direct foreign investment also tend to concentrate on those countries where economic growth and development indicate favorable performance and the international balance of payments shows no signs of uncertainty. In the case of Japan, private loans in the 1970s had represented a primary form of capital export made by the private sector. At the beginning of the 1980s, however, as the accumulated debt problem of Latin American countries surfaced and grew even worse, the share of private loans diminished. On the other hand, direct foreign investment from Japan since the early 1980s has been posting a substantial increase annually. The total amount of direct foreign investment in FY 1988 climbed to $47.3 billion and in FY 1989 to $67.5 billion, according to the statistics prepared by the Ministry of Finance. In comparison to the years of the 1970s, direct foreign investment from Japan to industrialized countries increased dramatically, while the weight of Japanese investment in developing countries decreased. In the 1970s, nearly 50 percent of Japan's direct foreign investment was directed to developing countries, but the statistics for FY 1989 show that the share dwindled to approximately 20 percent.

Japanese foreign direct investment for developed countries is concentrated mostly in the nonmanufacturing sectors, such as banking, security, and real estate. On the contrary, Japanese direct investment for developing countries is concentrated in the manufacturing industry. Furthermore, Japanese direct foreign investment for developing regions is also concentrated in Asia, especially in Asian NIEs and ASEAN countries. Since the end of the 1980s many Japanese manufacturers have started to establish "an international system of production" in the East and Southeast Asian economy (including the coastal region of China). These Japanese direct investments for Asia are strongly interdependent, with the expansion of manufactured goods being traded in terms of intraregional trade, intrafirm trade, intraindustry trade, and so on. Thus, in spite of a decline in the share of Japanese direct investment allocation, Asian countries can continue to benefit as the host economies.

The content of economic cooperation consists of various particulars. ODA, which is a main item of public funds, has multiple formulas, such as project-based assistance, technological cooperation, training of personnel, and even commodity loans and non–project-based assistance, to mention some. Furthermore, as one can see in recycling-of-funds programs, medium-income countries in the developing world, who are faced with an accumulated debt problem, may also be considered for significant economic and financial support.

The salient feature of such a type of cooperation is aimed, in large part, at alleviating difficulties in their international balance of payments; in principle, united funds are applied in this case. In addition, another key feature of this type of financial cooperation is that in most cases it falls into the category of non–project-based assistance.

In recent years, among the forms of economic cooperation, private-sector–initiated direct foreign investment is being highlighted. As mentioned earlier, the private sector's direct foreign investment is naturally based on the profitability of the project. It may not be fully consistent with economic cooperation in this respect. Yet, the flow of funds from the private sector to developing countries is receiving more attention due to its effect on employment, export promotion, technological transfer, and the solving of accumulated debt problems, among other things. In this context, mobilization of direct foreign investment led by the private sector is beginning to receive greater emphasis.

At any rate, in order to promote the flow of this type of assistance to developing countries, it is necessary to alleviate country risk and to build up economic systems on the part of recipients, among other things. The reason for the lesser flow of private direct foreign investment to third world debtor countries and LDCs is that the risks involved are considerably higher. Consequently, the governments of the investor and recipient countries alike must endeavor to improve the investment climate and to abate the risks of investment.

When viewed in terms of its relationship with capital exports, economic cooperation is increasingly rendered in diversified forms under the heading of capital exports, but in most cases, it combines a number of these forms. However, it is a fact that economic cooperation reflects the economic situation or international relations of the recipient developing country. In other words, with a country whose economy indicates a relatively low per-capita income level (below $500), ODA comprises the major part of economic cooperation since in these countries the construction of an economic infrastructure is being given the first priority.

When it comes to middle-income countries, not only ODA but also private direct foreign investment represents a more important part, in many cases. Most accumulated-debt–burdened countries are medium-income countries with a per-capita income level of over $1,000. They are not so suited to qualify as recipients of ODA; therefore it is often the case that the recycling of funds from Japan constitutes the most important part of economic cooperation.

On the other hand, there are also countries such as the Asian NIEs, who are no longer in need of ODA but are more concerned with technological transfer from Japan as a matter of future interest. Falling outside of capital exports and the abovementioned cooperation in the area of human resources, etc., provision of a Generalized System of Preference (GSP) represents another important form of economic cooperation classified under the subject of trade. But Asian NIEs are already "graduating" from this scheme and, in fact, the United States has already ceased to extend GSP to the Asian NIEs.

2. Criticism of Japanese Economic Cooperation

Up until the mid-1980s, Japan's economic cooperation received harsh criticism, which mainly focused on the following issues:

1. the level of funds for economic cooperation was inadequate;
2. the quality of economic cooperation was not sufficiently high;

3. assistance was mainly bilateral and very rarely multilateral; and
4. economic cooperation concentrates on specific regions.

When one studies Japan's performance in economic cooperation up to the middle of the 1980s, such criticism appears valid. Nevertheless, it should be pointed out that considerable improvements have been made in these problem areas since the mid-1980s, and continue to be made.

In light of the present, the following observations can be made with respect to these four issues. Regarding the level of economic cooperation funds, Japan's ODA in 1989 is considered to have reached the top of the list of ODA by the industrial countries of the world, in terms of absolute value on a disbursement basis. When compared to the nominal GNP for 1988, Japanese ODA accounted for 0.32 percent, which was surpassed only by the 0.8 percent achieved by Scandinavian countries. But, in comparison to the 0.39 percent of West Germany and the 0.32 percent of the United Kingdom, Japan may be said to have achieved a similar level of performance in ODA. The United States indicated a share of ODA of 0.21 percent, which was substantially below the Japanese share. In the case of Japan, improvement in terms of absolute value has been made to a greater extent than in terms of relative proportions of ODA in the total GNP. Incidentally, Japan's ODA embraces two elements. One is that ODA is granted a significantly high priority among the disbursement items in the government budget. This was especially true in the latter half of the 1980s. The other element was that the yen appreciated against the U.S. dollar during this period. This trend in the yen's exchange rate with respect to the dollar naturally served to push up the level of Japan's ODA, which was denominated in dollars. In other words, one should not forget that the yen's climb caused the expansion of ODA denominated in dollars far more than it made the yen-based ODA increase.

The criticism that the quality of Japanese economic cooperation is not high remains formidable even now. For example, the central pillar of Japan's economic cooperation consists of credits among ODA constituents. In fact, credits represent approximately 50 percent of the total ODA in the case of Japan, while in Great Britain or Sweden, grants represent 100 percent of their respective ODA components. In the United States and West Germany, the shares of grants in ODA represent 80 to 90 percent. In this respect, one cannot say that Japan's share of grants in ODA is adequate at present, compared with other industrial countries. As for other items under ODA, the portion of untied aid, for example, shows a higher percentage than that of other industrialized countries. Currently Japan's rate of untied aid is above 70 percent, which exceeds by far the 50 percent level of the United States and the 30 percent level of Italy.

It has been pointed out in past years that the weight of bilateral assistance is greater than that of multilateral assistance, or ODA extended to international institutions, in the case of Japan. In the case of the United States, the ratio of ODA directed to international institutions to the total ODA is 33 percent. The ratio for France is 18 percent, and West Germany's is 33 percent while Japan's is 30 percent. (All of the above are 1988 figures.) This means that Japan's performance is not exceptionally low. Recently, Japan has made remarkable advancements in capital subscription to the World Bank, and in contribution to the IMF Japan is now second only to the United States as a donor.

Finally, it has been a subject of criticism that Japanese economic cooperation concentrates on specific regions. It may be argued, however, that after World War II, Japan had begun to make reparations for war damages to Asian countries, and this is why Asia's share of Japanese ODA is extremely high. As a matter of fact, in the category of bilateral ODA, 98 percent of the total was channeled into Asian countries in 1970, but in 1987, Asia represented only 65 percent of the overall ODA. Such a shift may be considered drastic.

As I have delineated so far, economic cooperation by Japan, which is mainly comprised of ODA, has steadily progressed, with various improvements, since the middle of the 1980s, in spite of the number of problems that have been pointed out. In fact, some of the problems have been successfully overcome over the years. Yet one notes also that as diversification and expansion of economic cooperation in terms of fund amounts progressed, various new problems began to emerge. This is related to Japan's new role in the area of economic cooperation, and is linked also with its domestic structure.

3. Economic Cooperation Policy and Problem Areas of Domestic Structure

Economic cooperation policy has shifted in line with Japan's economic growth and role in the international community. Initially, Japanese eco-

nomic cooperation commenced with the extension of postwar reparations for war damages. In this respect, it was destined primarily for
Asian countries. This basic stance had been maintained throughout the
1960s and 1970s in conformity with the nation's foreign policy, which
attached greater importance to Asian countries.

Moreover, economic cooperation in those days was aimed at building
up the economic infrastructure of the recipient countries, which frequently involved Japanese exports, among other things. In this context,
one might say that economic cooperation by Japan in its earlier stages
was founded on economic motives. The first oil crisis (1973) in the
1970s had a dramatic impact on this stance toward economic cooperation. The oil crisis induced Japan to include part of the oil-exporting
countries in the Middle East as recipients of its economic cooperation.
Clearly, this was due to the policy decision by Japanese authorities to
place strong emphasis on securing natural resources, a salient political
factor.

Securing natural resources, naturally, is an economic factor as well,
but the fact remains that political implications prompted this priority
policy measure. In fact, this was the very first time that economic cooperation based on political factors/international relations was implemented.
One may describe this economic cooperation as something very close to
"strategic assistance." But to call it "strategic assistance" outright is
wrong, for this move lacked an aggressive and self-directed policy. It can
be said that the move was made in response to the oil-exporting policies
of the Middle East countries at that time.

Looking back, one sees that as Japan came to register large surpluses
in the current account balance in the 1980s—that is to say, as Japan
became exporter of capital and the scale of its economy sharply expanded—the United States moved from a broad current account balance
to a huge deficit, which posed the question of Japan taking on the role
of capital exporter in its turn.

Against this background, Japan's economic cooperation had to seek a
new direction. This new role had the implication that as the United
States, who had acted as a leader in the international economic system
in the postwar era, declined in weight and position, Japan, together with
West Germany, was obliged to assume the responsibility of maintaining
and developing the international economic system. The Maekawa Report was prepared with the aim of identifying Japan's role and tasks in
the international community from an immediate or short-term perspec-

tive. Concrete changes in policy have emerged in the area of economic cooperation since the mid-1980s. So far, improvements have been seen in the four problem areas mentioned earlier. In regard to deployment of "active strategic assistance," one observes that a rather "low-keyed strategic aid," or "passive strategic aid," seems to have had a stronger hand.

The basic reason for Japan's approach to economic cooperation being one of "passive strategic aid" is that although the amount of funds increased sharply and the pattern of economic cooperation became extremely diverse, provision of necessary arrangements such as effective coordination and/or division of labor among concerned government agencies was largely delayed. In fact, too many government agencies are involved with economic cooperation in Japan; most of them are in some way or another concerned with it. Specifically, four government agencies (Ministry of Finance, Ministry of Foreign Affairs, Ministry of International Trade and Industry, and the Economic Planning Agency) are in charge of this area. ODA is implemented as a result of consultation among these four government ministries, which is a domestic factor making economic cooperation even more complicated to undertake. Also, in a broader context, the acting body that is assigned to the extension of economic cooperation is comprised of several government financial institutions (e.g., the Overseas Economic Cooperation Funds, the Export-Import Bank of Japan, the International Cooperation Agency) that are staffed with a limited number of officers assigned with the actual service. The fact that this task is divided among several government agencies makes the system all the more complex. Presumably, there are overlapping investments and double investments in some cases. It should be pointed out also that for the past few years, economic cooperation has been given high priority in fiscal expenditure, so that every government ministry and agency is eagerly competing with each other to appropriate it in the budget. In other words, more than ever economic cooperation tends to be used as an instrument to secure budget allocation. A similar tendency can be seen on the political front, where the concept of "clans" has appeared with regard to government policies. For example, a "clan" interested in economic cooperation is beginning to take shape, making its appearance as an "economic cooperation interest group."

The Japanese people are becoming increasingly interested in economic cooperation, given its rise in terms of amount of funds since the end of the 1980s. As compared to previous years, the media have taken up this issue on many occasions. Nevertheless, economic cooperation is quite complicated with respect to its constituents, and its basic concept, among other things, is beyond the comprehension of ordinary people. In any event, there are countless black boxes defying the transparency in the realm of economic cooperation policy, and it is certain that problems will continue to arise one after another.

4. Direct Investment: Its Role and Its Problems

Japanese direct investment is focused upon as a means of economic cooperation. This manner of thinking existed historically, but recently it has been given more emphasis as being instrumental in promoting economic development in developing countries.

Direct investment includes capital, production technology, and management know-how in one single package, to be transferred to the recipient country. As a result, grading up of production technology and management know-how, including marketing among other things, expansion of employment, improvement of international balance of payments, etc., are expected to materialize in the recipient country. This is the reason why direct investment is emphasized as an instrument of economic cooperation. However, since direct investment by the private sector can be realized only as a result of the private sector's decision making, it requires profitability as a prerequisite for extension. In this context, private-sector–initiated direct investment does not always conform to the philosophy of economic cooperation.

Furthermore, the fact that private direct foreign investment sets viability as its precondition means that the relationships among markets, quality of labor (marginal productivity of labor), and wages must be erected within a certain framework of relations. As a consequence, direct foreign investment comes to be concentrated in a particular country. For example, unless there is basic political and social stability on the part of the host country, private-sector–initiated direct investment will not be introduced. In other words, among the means of economic cooperation, direct foreign investment may be utilized with a limited number of countries. Economic cooperation is directed to economics such as the

Asian NIEs or ASEAN countries, where performance in the area of economic development is seen as relatively favorable.

In view of such conditionalities, the donor country must thoroughly examine the role of private direct foreign investment and its effects on the recipient country. In this regard, effects on employment and other effects are relatively clear, while the role and effect of technological transfer are not readily visible. Developing countries place their expectations most eagerly on the effects of technological transfer. However, the technological transfer that is currently provided involves various problems.

In light of the present state of affairs, the problems that seem to require closest attention are (1) generalization of sophisticated technology in industrial countries; and (2) the progress of networking of international specialization.

The gap between the level of technology in industrial countries and that in developing countries is widening. Even if efforts were made by industrial countries to fill that gap, this would not be immediately possible. That is to say, the industrialized countries' level of technology is too far advanced, so that even if technology were transferred to developing countries, due to its capital-intensive nature and its sophistication, its industrially related impact over their domestic economies would be weak. The progress of international specialization in the network of technological transfer has the following implications: when private direct foreign investment is expanded in the context of the national economy of the recipient, the production of a specific area of industry becomes specialized. In other words, technological transfer for the production system in its entirety—that is, the production/management system, including management know-how—is an enormous task. Also, the progress of international specialization as the network of technological transfer might even serve as an obstacle.

In this manner, various reservations exist for the utilization of private direct foreign investment as a vehicle of economic cooperation. But it is only natural for different methods of economic cooperation to be more effective in different countries in various developmental stages. It is also a fact that private-sector–initiated direct investment performs a significant role in the recipient country, in many instances. In such cases, the host country should make necessary adjustments so as to avoid investment conflicts with the donor country as much as possible, or should design the kind of channeling of funds that will prevent them from arising. To take the example of the recent increase of Japan's import of manufactured products, Japan tends to import from particular countries (such as ASEAN countries), and this gives rise to a serious shortfall in infrastructure in other developing countries. In this instance, extending economic cooperation to provide the country with the bottleneck infrastructure will certainly be effective in resolving the issue. Since the destination (region) for direct foreign investment led by the private sector is basically decided through consideration of relations between profits and risks, the recipient country is well advised to take some policy steps (which could be preferential measures) to alleviate the potential risks to the investors to promote investment. Such policy measures will bring forth results similar to subsidies, and are likely to distort the recipient's market mechanism. At any rate, it appears that the role of private direct foreign investment in the area of economic cooperation remains only supplementary.

5. Economic and Industrial Cooperation for Eastern Europe and Russia

The dramatic moves toward democratization and changes in the political regimes that swept Eastern Europe in 1989 presented an important question to Japan's economic cooperation. Eastern European countries naturally need investment funds for reconstruction of their economies; and the portion that exceeds domestic savings must be procured from abroad, through the vehicles of assistance, public and private loans, and direct foreign investment, among others. The Japanese government is trying to actively respond to such essential requests from Eastern Europe. Already, it has committed its financial cooperation to Hungary and Poland, and decided to make a capital subscription to the European Bank for Reconstruction and Development. This will be in the amount of close to $2 billion as a relief package for Eastern Europe, according to the official announcement. Such economic and financial cooperation may be considered extremely prompt in comparison to past processing of Japanese policy measures for economic cooperation. It is also distinctly noteworthy with respect to political factors and international relations. In the private sector also, industrial cooperation based on direct investment and the transfer of technology is underway, and primarily will made available to Hungary, Czechoslovakia, and Poland. In Hungary, for example, actual projects are beginning to be launched. These moves by Japanese corporations are at the same time becoming a cause of concern and wariness on the part of Western Europe. Nevertheless, it is not likely that Japanese corporations will make large-scale direct foreign investments in the short term to Eastern European countries. That is because political and social stability and the rebuilding of various systems, which constitute preconditions for direct investment, are not yet in order in the region. These are yet to come. There may be lags to varying degrees, depending upon the individual country involved, but direct investment in East Europe will probably be looked at in the medium and long terms.

In the case of Russia, on the grounds of political considerations there has been no significant progress in Japan-Soviet economic and industrial cooperation. The issue of the four Northern Islands will have an important bearing on this front. There should be no progress made in the area of cooperation unless it is preceded by progress with the Northern Islands issue. In any event, solving the political issues between Japan and Russia must come first, before economic and industrial cooperation between the two countries shows any sign of moving forward. However, Russia is in the middle of confusion and difficulties. The country has registered negative economic growth and is enduring extreme hardships. On the other hand, in the context of supply of natural resources, among other things, the Soviet economy and the Japanese economy could be in a complementary relationship in the long term. It could be said that, in the long run, both countries have economic reasons to form cooperative economic and industrial relations. In the event that various political issues between Japan and the Soviet Union are resolved, government-based financial cooperation will be most urgent in the short run, as is the case in Eastern European countries. When this happens it will also be important to incorporate Russia into an international economic system. One might say that this is one of the preconditions for the improvement of Japan-Russia relations.

6. Economic Cooperation with China

Starting with the authorization of the First Yen Loan to China in 1980, Japan made available to the People's Republic of China gratuitous and nongratuitous contracts, technological transfers, private-sector-led financial cooperation, and direct foreign investment, under the heading of economic cooperation.

Under the open door policy in China since 1978, Japanese economic and financial cooperation with China has been implemented mainly through the provision of an economic infrastructure and the development of natural resources for export.

In the meantime, China aggressively liberalized its economy after 1978 and achieved high economic growth and trade expansion. Then, in the latter half of the 1980s, various problems began to emerge, among which inflation was a serious cause for anxiety. After 1988, economic adjustment policy steps were taken in 1989, and the Tiananmen Square Incident broke out. Ever since, Japan has suspended authorization of yen credits to China. In fact, no signs of progress are seen in the area of official financial cooperation to that country. A similar stance is taken by countries in the West, as well as by international financial institutions such as the IBRD.

From 1990 to 1991, the Japanese government examined this matter and decided to reopen Japanese ODA and financial cooperation with China from the point of view of "averting the isolation of China."

At present, economic cooperation with China has developed into a highly political consideration. In the medium to long term, the overall picture may be different. Currently, however, China is a country that embraces the world's largest population, with a per-capita income of approximately $400. There is an enormous regional gap between the coastal region, where economic liberalization is advanced and the inhabitants are relatively well off, and the economically underdeveloped inland region. It is a country burdened with various difficulties. Yet, geographically it is close to Japan, and needless to say, China is an important country for Japan. In the medium and long term, therefore, Japan should proceed with economic cooperation in compliance with the principle of "extending indirect support for the self-reliant efforts of developing countries." Given that the Chinese economy shows diversified faces, economic cooperation ought to combine various forms of assistance to satisfy its needs. For example, private direct foreign investment will presumably have a greater role to play in the coastal region which is the center of liberalized economic policy measures. Also, it is considered that in many cases ODA is relatively better suited to the investment climate of the coastal region. In addition, there will be future needs for economic cooperation on environmental projects. In any event, China is faced with all sorts of worries in the short term, which present hurdles to economic cooperation. In the medium and long term, China will definitely require it in varying forms and in a fairly sizeable amount.

7. Recycling of Funds to Third World Debtors

The crises that occurred in the early 1980s in the international balance of payments of medium-income countries, particularly those of Latin American countries, deteriorated further despite the efforts of industrial and debtor countries. In the latter half of the 1980s, once again, the accumulated debt problem had to be coped with by the use of drastic measures, including reduction of outstanding principal and interest rates. The situation urgently requires new developments. Since 1987, Japan has been making commitments to financial cooperation with these countries. This recycling of funds was first decided upon by the Nakasone administration and was implemented more in collaboration with the United States than on the initiative of Japan itself. In this context, it was clearly tinged with political and international relations concerns, though it was economic financial cooperation. Such commitment has other important implications than just that of collaboration with the United States. For example, preservation of the international monetary system can be cited. Nevertheless, this also entails a number of problems. Repayment of past loans by private financial institutions, including repayment of principal and payment of interest, is also made possible through financial cooperation. In other words, such a case could be interpreted as shifting the obligations of accumulated-debt–ridden countries from the private sector to the public sector. In addition, financial cooperation of this nature is mainly directed toward supporting the international balance of payments on a nonproject basis. For this reason, financial cooperation by the World Bank and the IMF is conditional on certain prerequisites, such as adoption of macroeconomic policies to restore the economy and modification of related policies including monetary, trade, industrial, and privatization policies. Japan also will put forth terms and conditions that approximate those of the IMF or IBRD. In fact, Japan has not quoted its own terms and conditions for credit extension as yet. The major reason for this is that the shortage of staff, among other things, prevents the domestic system from being fully equipped. This is another problem area that needs to be addressed in the future. As opposed to the type of economic cooperation extended in the past, which centered around a given project, financial cooperation to third world debtor countries may involve many aspects that are not readily comprehensible. Especially, it is difficult to assess how the economic cooperation program has progressed, and to what extent its goals can be achieved. Most of the data currently in use is kept confidential, and that is why a substantial part of it is known as being in a "black box." Hopefully, in the future, a public record will be kept regarding how financial cooperation of this type was prepared beforehand, how it was implemented, and, in the process, what kind of role was played by the Japanese government financial institutions involved.

8. The Need for National Consensus

Presumably, Japan's commitment to economic and financial cooperation in the 1990s will continue to operate at the highest level in the world. In 1989, the consumption tax introduced by the government aroused heated debate across the country. Even though it falls short of 1 percent of GNP, Japanese economic and financial cooperation still constitutes a vast sum of money. Since about 1989, increasing interest in this subject has begun to be shown by the people. The media have taken it up as a topic of discussion, and gradually, related materials have been published. It is often found that economic and financial cooperation involves complicated issues that are difficult for the people to fully understand. However, because of the sharp increase in the amount of such cooperation, it seems natural that the actual state of affairs and problems have been highlighted. Unless more adequate understanding of, and support for, this area of cooperation can be obtained from the Japanese people in general, Japan will be unable to play an active role in the international community. In short, in the 1990s, soliciting national consensus on this issue will become essential.

The constituents of national consensus may be as follows:

1. it is necessary to agree on the basic philosophy of economic and financial cooperation (international relations and political elements should be taken into account to a greater extent);

2. it is necessary to agree on the expansion of funds and related institutions aimed at economic and financial cooperation (this refers mainly to domestic institutions);
3. it is necessary to agree on the method of allocation of funds for this purpose ("allocation" in this case refers to allocation by region and by country as well as by area and by target);
4. as to assessing the effect of cooperation, the people should be able to know the results of that assessment;
5. overall, "transparency" of economic and financial cooperation must be enhanced; and
6. agreement on the importance of economic and financial cooperation is necessary.

As the people's interest in cooperation heightens, voices of criticism may also arise. Some of these voices are appropriate, constructive, and positive, while some others are clearly derived from misunderstanding. The Japanese government and related institutions ought to accept those voices that need to be accepted but counter other voices that must definitely be countered. It is only after going through this basic process that national consensus or understanding can be gained.

9. Policy Priorities for Specific Economic and Financial Cooperation

Policy priorities may be classified into two categories: those that must be coped with in the short term and those that should be tackled in the medium and long terms. There is one other type of classification that we can distinguish: policy priorities concerning methods of cooperation— in other words, specifications or particulars of cooperation—as opposed to policy priorities concerning Japan's domestic structure as it is involved in extending cooperation.

As for the latter, it should be noted that in some cases cooperation under this heading needs to be enhanced as a "grant" whereas in other cases it ought to be processed in the form of "untied" aid. For example, it has already been pointed out that mobilization of aid in an "untied" form is substantially utilized by other industrial countries. Under the heading of "LDC untied" aid, however, joint venture companies involving Japanese investors and the host country's entrepreneurs have an increasingly larger share of the total procurement. Yet, these being joint venture companies, the host country side naturally has the majority share in the ownership of these de facto local companies. For this reason, the host side often holds a grudge against the investor side, and such a form of cooperation cannot be considered "untied" in substance. In view of the circumstances, it is necessary to take a more positive stance in extending economic cooperation that is "untied" in substance as well.

There are also some serious problems that are beginning to be seen in the area of technological cooperation. It is said that, in regard to this area, the kind of technological cooperation that can be made available to developing countries is fast disappearing from Japan, so that in the near future, technological transfer may become an area in which international cooperation is no longer possible. That is to say, Japan has moved to such a sophisticated level of technology overall that it no longer will have any stock of technology that developing countries actually require. In this context, it is essential for Japan to proceed with coordination with the developing world and the Asian NIEs, among other countries, in the areas of economic cooperation and technological transfer. What this points to is that Japan alone may not be able to accommodate the needs of the developing world in these areas. Such a possibility is arising from the change in Japan's stock of technology.

On the other hand, building up Japan's domestic structure poses the greatest task in the realm of economic and financial cooperation. Especially in such areas as analyzing and reviewing the effects of cooperation, both human resources and capital are lacking. This applies to both macroeconomic and microeconomic analyses. In addition, continuation of the complicated domestic structure concerned with cooperation poses difficulties. It will be necessary to set up a new system, including restructuring the existing government financial institutions (implementing body), which utilize a small number of staff as much as possible. At present, some of the content of work overlaps, being carried out by a number of implementing bodies in many cases.

Another point to be noted is that in the 1990s utilization of the private sector will be an important task. Utilization of this private sector may appear contradictory to the plea for untying the aid. Consequently, concerned parties should be careful in their use of the private sector to ensure that no contradiction in such regard will arise. That is to say, taking into account the shortage of human resources in the public sector and the draining away of the kind of technology from Japan that developing countries need, Japan ought to enhance its utilization of skilled laborers who are advanced in age as well as cooperation with the private sector.

In closing, we must remind ourselves of three aspects of Japan's economic and financial cooperation in connection with its role in the international community in the 1990s. The first aspect concerns the world as a whole and is related to the GATT and the international monetary regime. The second aspect is related to regional cooperation. We should be careful in extending economic and financial cooperation so that the above two questions do not mutually contradict each other. In this context, much will depend on what role Japan will assume in the international arena in the 1990s in the area of economic and financial cooperation. This will be the basic vision on which drafting, planning, and implementing policies addressing the above will be based.

The third aspect is the possibility of Japan as a model of the development experience. Since the 1970s, we have had some successful stories of economic development in Asia. There are several factors in common between Japanese development experiences and the recent success stories in Asia, some of which will apply to other developing countries such as Latin American and East European countries as well as the USSR. This makes it more important that we initiate, on our own, intensive research on and study of the Japanese economic development experience, in light of future economic and financial cooperation for developing countries.

Finally, I would like to point out that in the 1990s Japan should pursue a "Japanese way of economic and financial cooperation." The new Japanese way should take into account two points at least. These are (1) offering information on our past experiences and on Japanese economic development (including the past economic development experiences of other Asian countries) and (2) adopting clear criteria based on human rights and social, political, and military elements.

The Japanese experience of long-term economic development since the Meiji Restoration and after World War II, and some other Asian success experiences, are unlike many Western economies' development and growth experiences with regard to several points, such as manner of working the market price, formation of the market, the relationship between business and government, priority sectors in the process of economic development, and so on. To evolve a new Japanese style of economic and financial cooperation in the 1990s, we should intensively allocate more human resources to this field and should mobilize strong multilateral cooperation among groups such as the academic community (joint work between economists, political scientists, and scholars of international relations), the business community, and the public sector.

The Japanese way will have to be different from the existing method used by the United States, the United Kingdom, France, and Scandinavia. The basic requirements will have to take into account peacekeeping, arms reduction, human rights, a clearer political element, and a reflection of Japanese development experiences. Since the Gulf War, the LDP (Liberal Democratic party) of Japan has started to discuss seriously Japan's new strategic aid, which takes into account peacekeeping, arms reduction, and democratization in host countries. This issue will be one of the most important problems that many Japanese should consider in the 1990s.

Notes

1. *World Debt Tables 1990,* World Bank, 1991.
2. *Balance of Payments Monthly,* Bank of Japan, April 1992.

References

Development Assistance Committee (DAC). *Development Cooperation: 1990 Report.* Paris: OECD, 1991.

Ministry of Foreign Affairs of Japan. *Japan's Official Development Assistance: 1990 Annual Report.* Tokyo, 1990.

Ministry of International Trade and Industry of Japan. *Present Situation and Issues in Economic Cooperation, 1989.* Tokyo, 1990.

Orr, Robert M. *The Emergence of Japan's Foreign Aid Power.* New York: Columbia University Press, 1990.

Shafiqul, Islam, ed. *Yen for Development: Japanese Foreign Aid and the Politics of Burden Sharing.* New York: Council on Foreign Relations, 1991.

Yasutomo, Dennis T. *The Manner of Giving: Strategic Aid and Japanese Foreign Policy.* Lexington, Mass.: Heath, 1986.

6. Japan's International Agenda: Structural Adjustments

Heizo Takenaka

Since the release of the Maekawa Report in 1986, the term "structural adjustment" has become a key phrase in discussions of issues and policies regarding the Japanese economy. There should be no need to mention the importance of promoting the international harmonization of macroeconomic policies in ameliorating external imbalances among the leading industrial nations, particularly between Japan and the United States. Furthermore, awareness has been growing among Japanese and foreign policy analysts of the need for structural changes to the societies and economies of Japan and the United States. This awareness has strengthened among mainstream analysts and policymakers as those few who stress that Japan is uniquely different from Europe and the United States have gained visibility in recent years.

As economic globalization progresses, it is both necessary and vitally important that Japan's society and economy develop a structure that is compatible with those of other nations. Many also hope this process will improve the economic well-being of Japanese citizens. Furthermore, since all leading industrial nations need to undertake economic structural adjustments based on international harmonization, it will be beneficial for Japan to assume a leadership role in this process. For these reasons, Japan's basic support for structural adjustments has been clearly evident among government, industry, and consumers.

Nevertheless, many problems are still associated with economic structural adjustments. What exactly do structural adjustments consist of? Are their effects major or minor? What practical government policy measures are required? Based on these questions, this paper will clarify what meaning structural adjustments hold for the Japanese economy and will discuss an agenda for achieving these adjustments.

First, Japan's need for economic structural adjustments and the importance of diminishing the spread between domestic and foreign prices will be examined. Next, three areas where change is needed—land, distribution markets, and the competitiveness of Japanese markets—will be analyzed. Finally, the need for basic social and economic reform in realizing suitable structural adjustments will be emphasized.

1. The Need for Structural Adjustments

The world economy experienced unprecedented changes in the latter half of the 1980s. Financial services and such factors of production as capital and labor began to move easily across national borders. The activities of corporations and consumers began to encompass the entire globe. As a result of economic "globalization," small differences in national economic policies and economic systems could trigger sudden and substantial cross-border shifts in product flows and in factors of production. This has the potential of destabilizing world markets. "Black Monday," or the stock market collapse of October 1987, brought into sharp relief the degree to which interdependence governed the world and could shake markets.

Another major development was the Plaza Accord of 1985, which sparked the yen's considerable appreciation against the dollar. This did not, however, initially result in a substantial decline of Japan's current account surplus. For this and other reasons, some in the United States have declared that Japan's social and economic system is unique and have criticized Japan on this basis. The debate on this among specialists continues, but whatever its outcome, the need for Japan to undertake economic structural adjustments in order to better harmonize with the world has become widely accepted. The ambiguous meaning of "structural adjustments," nevertheless, has hampered constructive debate and policy actions.

"Structural adjustment" is quite a convenient phrase. Economists commonly identify as structural those features that remain unchanged for long periods of time. Some therefore label all changes to long-term phenomena as structural changes. There are, on the other hand, those that hold that structural change is impossible since "structure" by definition refers to unchanging phenomena. Therefore, providing a proper definition for "structural adjustment" is difficult. From the perspective of the economic discipline, one cannot immediately conclude that structural changes or structural adjustments have taken place when changes to economic variables bring about a change in economic structure. For example, suppose that Japan's share of manufactured imports in total import volume rises as a result of the yen's appreciation. Any economy has the propensity for manufactured imports to rise by a certain percentage when the national currency strengthens. Therefore, when imports increase as the yen appreciates, this change is not necessarily a structural adjustment but may be just a normal economic adjustment. However, should some factor cause the very propensity to import to rise and consequently change the amount of imports by more or less than the usual, this can be labeled as a structural adjustment.

Thus, structural adjustments can be defined as changes to the structural parameters that are built into the economy. These changes often depend on alterations in social and economic phenomena. For example, systemic changes in import procedures, changes to the means by which foreign currency rate fluctuations are manifested in domestic prices, and variations of demand function configurations arising from changes in consumer values would mark the occurrence of structural adjustment.[1]

Reflecting the complex nature of the difficulties associated with structural adjustment issues, most of the leading industrial nations have been reluctant to promote structural adjustment of their economies. Japan is the only nation to have announced a clear plan of action, as represented by the Maekawa Report.[2]

Structural adjustment plays an important role for Japan's government, industry, and consumers. First, it is recognized that structural adjustments will help enormously in ameliorating external imbalances among leading industrial nations, particularly between Japan and the United States. A simulation analysis of a global economic model[3] indi-

Table 6.1 Simulating Policy Changes: Divergences from the Base Line

	Japan (A) Rate of GNP Growth (Average 1991–1995)	Japan (B) Ratio of Trade Balance to GNP (1995)	U.S.A. (A)	U.S.A. (B)	Asian NIEs (A)	Asian NIEs (B)
Case I	0.4	-0.6	0	1.1	0.7	-0.1
Case II	3.5	-1.9	0.2	1.7	2.5	0

Source: H. Takenaka, *Nichibei Masatsu no Keizaigaku* (Economics on U.S.–Japan Frictions), Tokyo: Nihon Keizai Shimbun, 1991.

cates that divergence of Japanese and U.S. macroeconomic policies (i.e., the growth of U.S. budget deficits and Japan's austerity efforts) was the principal factor in the expansion of the U.S. trade deficit between 1980 and 1985, accounting for 60 percent of the trade deficits the United States accumulated during that time. The remaining 40 percent depended on the increasing income elasticity of U.S. import demand, reflecting the declining savings rate and various other structural factors. Furthermore, only 32 percent of Japan's external surpluses of the same period were explained by changes in macroeconomic policies. The remainder likely depended on various structural changes such as changes in savings and investment behavior. This therefore suggests the need for both harmonization of macroeconomic policies (i.e., reduction of the U.S. budget deficit and expansion of Japan's domestic demand) and structural adjustments to make significant improvements to the external imbalances of Japan and the United States.

A more recent simulation analysis suggests that carrying out structural adjustments through the 1990s will be indispensable in ameliorating external imbalances and in ensuring the stable management of the world economy. Table 6.1 indicates the outcome of simulation of using a small model of the global economy to determine the results of macroeconomic policy coordination among Japan, the United States, and Europe (Case 1) and the results of the addition of structural adjustments to macroeconomic policy coordination (Case 2) (the figures represent the difference between each case and the baseline situation of taking no policy action at all). Case 1 assumes that the United States lowers government expenditure growth by 1 percent from the baseline and that Japan and other OECD nations lift their government expenditure growth by 1 percent. Case 2 presumes that, in addition to the macroeconomic policies of Case 1, structural changes to the Japanese economy push consumer prices down and that existing differences in domestic and foreign prices are about halved in five years. In other words, Case 2 assumes that a decline in the level of domestic prices will increase the purchasing power of Japanese consumers and boost the expansion of domestic demand. Table 6.1 makes clear that the combination of macroeconomic policy coordination and structural adjustments, as in Case 2, has a far greater effect than the Case 1 situation in promoting domestic and foreign economic growth and in improving external imbalances. Particularly noteworthy is Case 2's efficacy in bolstering the growth of the Asian NIEs. Domestically, there are many who believe that structural adjustments are an effective means for responding to the criticism that Japan is uniquely different, but who fear adjustments would be ineffectual in promoting economic growth or improving external imbalances. Table 6.1 nevertheless shows that structural adjustments would have a sizable economic effect, both domestically and internationally. What must be stressed at this point is the importance of economic structural adjustments not only for Japan but for all leading industrial nations. For example, the amelioration of external imbalances on a global scale will only begin to take place when Japan bolsters domestic demand through structural adjustments and, complementarily, the United States carries out such structural changes as lifting its private-sector savings rate and strengthening the supply side of its economy.

A second reason why structural adjustments are important for Japan lies in the fact that many of the anticipated specific changes will help improve the economic well-being of Japanese citizens over the medium and long term. For this reason, policies and issues discussed in the Maekawa Report and other documents ought to be pursued, regardless of their effectiveness in ameliorating external economic relations, since they support the general goal of economic policy, the realization of comfortable lives for citizens. A number of factors, such as the shortening of working hours, the further liberalization of imports, the control of real estate prices, or the streaming of the distribution system, will all contribute to the improvement of the national economy. Consequently, despite the vagueness associated with the concept of structural adjustments, it represents an important prescription for dealing with both domestic and external policy issues. This prospect has already attracted considerable interest in Japan and its importance will only increase in the 1990s.

With economic interdependence markedly increasing, the stable management of the global economy will require the international coordination of structural adjustment policies as well as the coordination of macroeconomic policies. Discussions concerning the coordination of macroeconomic policies have taken place repeatedly at economic summits and at the Group of Five and Group of Seven meetings of finance ministers and central bankers. These discussions have engendered a certain amount of success. Moreover, multilateral surveillance of national economic policies and economic performance has occurred since the Tokyo Summit of 1986, which has strengthened the framework for international coordination. As far as economic structural adjustments are concerned, one can point to the recent conclusion of the bilateral Structural Impediments Initiative discussions between Japan and the United States. As has been stated above, the coordination of macroeconomic policies will only be effective when it takes place in tandem with economic structural adjustments. Japan's economic structural adjustments, first elaborated in the Maekawa Report, have been conceived within such a global framework.

2. Domestic and Foreign Price Differences

Adjustments to economic structures can take place in a variety of ways, and it is extremely difficult to develop uniform indicators to reveal the existence of individual problems and their relative size. However, the spread in prices between domestic Japanese markets and foreign markets, or differences in domestic and foreign prices, can be viewed as the expression of a variety of structural problems. If international transactions take place without exposure to structural barriers and if domestic markets are without structural distortion, domestic price levels should mirror international levels.

An effective means of comparing domestic and foreign prices is found by weighing purchasing price parity against current foreign exchange rates. Table 6.2 compares Japan's price levels with other nations based

Table 6.2 OECD Purchasing Power Parity and Japan's Price Level
(1989)

	(A) P.P.P.	(B) Exchange Rate	(A)/(B) Japanese Price Level*
U.S.A.	196.0	138.0	142
W. Germany	84.6	73.4	115
France	26.7	21.6	124
U.K.	314.0	226.0	139

* Price level of a particular country = 100
Source: Economic Planning Agency, Bukka Repoto 90 (Price Report 90), Tokyo: Economic Planning Agency, 1990.

on HOE figures for the purchasing price parity of consumer goods. The table reveals that Japanese prices are two times that of the United States and 1.2 to 1.4 times that of major European nations.

Japan's Economic Planning Agency has also made an international comparison of prices for individual products. The agency took four hundred of the most important products constituting the consumer price index and compared their prices in Tokyo, New York, and Hamburg in November 1988 (using the exchange rates of that time to convert prices). It reported that prices in Tokyo exceeded those in New York and Hamburg by 1.16 and 1.20 times, respectively (Economic Planning Agency [1990]). While the outcomes of these two studies diverge slightly, one cannot deny that Japanese price levels surpass international levels by a significant margin.

Several problems, nevertheless, are associated with the international comparison of prices. First, there is the possibility that foreign exchange rates deviate from appropriate levels when comparisons are made. For example, even if surveys disclose that Japanese prices eclipse those in the United States, this could merely be the result of the yen being over-valued against the dollar. Second, differences could exist in the composition of goods purchased by Japanese and foreign consumers—a problem that is part of all price comparisons. Third, differences in price levels among nations do not necessarily mean that structural distortions exist. The economic theory of prices states that similar corporations manufacturing analogous goods will set prices high in countries with low price elasticity of demand and will set prices low in countries with high price elasticity. This behavior is the rational outcome of seeking to maximize profits.

Despite the problems that are associated with the international comparison of prices, it is significant that Japan's price levels surpass those of Europe and the United States by 20 to 40 percent. Japan's real income would therefore rise by 20 to 40 percent if domestic prices dropped to international levels. (Many have pointed out the need to distinguish between merchandise trade goods and nonmerchandise trade goods in regard to the spread between domestic and foreign prices. Such differentiation is theoretically proper.) The spread between domestic and foreign prices is said to be large for nonmerchandise trade goods and small for merchandise trade goods. If that is the case, why Japan's nonmerchandise trade goods are so expensive and why the spread in prices between Japan's merchandise trade and nonmerchandise trade account is so wide relative to other nations are questions that demand ready answers.

What factors account for Japan's high price levels? While it is difficult to point to a single, clear factor, five basic reasons can be cited.

First, certain production input prices are high in Japan. For example, real estate prices and rents are high, reflecting Japan's small geographic size; and oil and other energy input prices are high since the nation lacks many natural resources. These factors will not be easy to surmount.

Second, some have argued that Japan's distribution system is inefficient, curbing competition. The validity of this argument will be discussed later.

Third, the prices of some imported products are higher domestically than overseas. This is particularly conspicuous for agricultural products under strict import regulations.

Fourth, the prices of some Japanese exports are higher domestically than overseas. Cameras, televisions, and film are frequently cited examples. It is not clear, however, how important this is overall.

Fifth, some international services (e.g., international air fares) are higher when originating in Japan than when originating overseas. This particular spread between Japanese and foreign prices remains large.

Of the five factors just cited, Japanese experts do not agree on which is the most important or on the extent to which each factor accounts for the spread in domestic and foreign prices. One thing, nevertheless, is certain. These differences in domestic and foreign prices can be viewed as a list of problems that points to the existence of distortions of one form or another within Japan's economy. By eliminating the spread in domestic and foreign prices or by correcting the social distortions that cause them, Japanese consumers will be able more fully to enjoy the results of their national economic development.

3. Individual Issues

The structural adjustments Japan's economy is experiencing reflect a range of issues. Six issues were raised at the Structural Impediments Initiative (SII) talks between the Japanese and U.S. governments: (1) savings and investment patterns, (2) land usage, (3) distribution, (4) exclusionary business practices, (5) *keiretsu* or affiliate relationships, and (6) the price mechanism. Of these, (1) is an issue of macroeconomic policy, and (6) can be considered the consolidation of all other structural problems. Furthermore, (4) and (5) both concern the overall competitiveness of Japan's markets. I will consequently examine two more pertinent issues: land problems and distribution markets, and the issue of competitiveness of Japanese markets, offering possible prescriptions.

Land Problems

Rocketing land prices have been an ongoing problem confronting the Japanese economy since the conclusion of World War II. Although Japan's consumer price index has risen some fivefold in the last thirty years, land prices in six large cities (residential areas) have spurted 155-fold on the average. Real estate prices climbed unusually rapidly in the 1970s and 1980s. As a result, it became all but impossible for ordinary Japanese citizens to purchase new homes. Currently, the price of a home corresponds to 7.5 times the annual average income of a Japanese person (Tokyo area). This surpasses by a wide margin the comparable figures of 3.4, 4.4, and 4.6 times, respectively, for the United States, Great Britain, and West Germany (Real Estate Economic Institute survey). Furthermore, swelling real estate values have widened the income gap between those who own property and those who do not, raising concern about this gap's potential to dampen the will to work over the long term. The value of real estate owned by individual households appreciated 36.0 trillion yen between 1986 and 1988. Such colossal capital gains, fully matching the size of Japan's GNP, fell into the laps of only those citizens with real estate holdings, approximately 60 percent of Japan's population. The result was an enormous gap in asset income between property holders and the remaining 40 percent without any claim to property.

Surging real estate prices also affect Japan's savings and investment balance. Rising real estate values have significantly reduced the effective outlays of public works spending. The National Land Agency's National Land Use White Paper for 1988 reports that 99 percent of the total outlays for major road projects in Tokyo's Minato and Chiyoda wards was spent on land acquisitions. Rocketing land prices can therefore be perceived as reducing public capital formation when measured by Japan's national accounts. On the other hand, the real estate problem has contributed to excess private savings through two routes and has become a factor bolstering Japan's current account surplus. First, it has raised the target amount for the purchase of a home that is placed in savings, thereby contributing to the considerable size of household savings. Previous analysis has confirmed that one-half to two-thirds of Japanese household savings are set aside for the purpose of acquiring a home. Second, the real estate problem has also put a brake on housing investment over the medium and long terms. Housing investment accounted for 7 percent of Japan's GNP in the 1970s, a figure that dropped to about 5 percent in the 1980s. (Nevertheless, the ascent of real estate and other asset values has boosted the consumption expenditures of asset holders through the so-called wealth effect and has helped to diminish Japan's current account surplus.)

Although Japan's small geographic size is frequently cited as a reason for the nation's high real estate prices, this is not an acceptable explanation. The problem is that real estate is held not as a means of production but for speculative purposes, meaning that property is not put to effective use. As an example, a National Land Agency (1988) estimate indicates that even though the average legal building capacity ratio (total floor area to site area) in Tokyo's twenty-three wards came to 242 percent as of 1986, the actual building capacity ratio was only 95 percent. If property holdings were put to use up to the maximum permitted building capacity ratio, the resulting floor space would be sufficient to house the total population of Tokyo's twenty-three wards (8.4 million people) as well as all commuters and their families (5.4 million).

An immediate factor in Japan's surging real estate values is the extremely limited supply of land, despite the existence of strong demand for private homes and office space. The area of land that is actually traded annually does not even come to 1 percent of Japan's real estate stock, a situation that is distorting the formation of real estate prices. Yukio Noguchi has demonstrated that the market price of Japan's real estate equals two to three times its theoretical value.[4] (The theoretical value is determined by taking all future expected rent income and discounting such income to its present value.) Property taxes must therefore be raised as well as capital gains taxes on property transfers in order to expand the supply of real estate. The Japanese government, however, has substantially reduced the taxable assessed values of real estate to lessen the property taxes paid by individuals and has lifted the capital gains tax on property transfers to thwart real estate speculation. Currently, the effective tax rate on real estate has fallen to 0.19 percent and the maximum capital gains tax on property transfers (including local taxes) has risen to 85.2 percent.

Many economists agree on the desirability of lifting property taxes and lowering capital gains taxes on property transfers to ensure that the market functions properly in establishing real estate prices. Nevertheless, previous analyses, though few in number, suggest that the effectiveness of such a policy will likely depend on increasing current property taxes from ten to fifty times, perhaps even higher. Such a change will not find ready political acceptance. A 1988 public opinion survey conducted by the prime minister's office reveals that 42 percent of Japanese citizens would like to see property taxes reduced and only 4 percent believe that they should be raised. Since 62 percent of Japan's total housing stock consists of owner-occupied houses, a majority of Japanese citizens realize capital gains when real estate values climb. This situation impedes the implementation of effective land policy.

A major revision of Japan's tax system, headed by a significant increase in property taxes, can offer a way out of the real estate impasse. In this process, it will be also be necessary to implement the following policies in a comprehensive manner.

- Revise the Land and House Rent Law, which currently favors renters, and thereby promote the efficient use of real estate.
- Ease regulations regarding building capacity ratios.
- Disperse and transfer various capital city functions (including the possibility of relocating the capital) to curb the growth of demand for real estate in the greater Tokyo region.

As a first step toward implementing the above measures, farm lands in urbanizing districts should be taxed at the same rate as residential property, an action that has long been under consideration.

The Distribution Market

Japan's distribution system is complicated and hard to understand, creating a barrier for foreign corporations wishing to participate in the domestic market. Many contend that the system keeps retail prices high and thereby dampens domestic demand. How does Japan's distribution market compare with those of foreign nations? The OECD's *Economic Survey: Japan 1987/88* shows that the density of retail and wholesale outlets (ratio of stores to a given number of population) is higher in Japan than in other major HOE nations and that the channels of distribution have many more tiers.

In *Distribution System and Business Practices in Japan,* a publication of the Economic Planning Agency's Economic Research Institute (1989), we see that Japan's distribution system is characterized as having a greater number of smaller retail stores and additional tiers of wholesalers when compared with other nations. Even so, the publication maintains that there is economic justification for this. The greater number of smaller-sized retail stores is a reflection of consumers who demand fresh food, shop frequently for small quantities because of a shortage of storage space at home, and expect speedy delivery and after-sale service. The high cost of inventory also abets the current retail structure. Furthermore, Japan's multitiered wholesale system arises out of its retail structure of large numbers of small outlets. Since there is a limit to how many business relations one wholesaler can maintain, other wholesalers come in between to consolidate transaction units and to reduce the size of business networks. According to the publication, this system lowers the costs for both manufacturers and retailers of placing and receiving orders.

The Economic Research Institute has estimated the margin rate for the domestic multitiered wholesale system as a whole and has compared that rate with equivalent figures from other nations to determine the overall efficiency of Japan's distribution margin. It came to 57.6 percent, somewhat higher than the United States' 49.7 percent, but fully comparable to the figures of other major industrial nations (West Germany,

58.9 percent; Great Britain, 55.6 percent; and France, 55.3 percent). The inventory turnover of Japan's distribution system as a whole showed no less efficiency than that of the United States and other major industrial nations.

Several points can be raised regarding the Economic Research Institute study. First, if Japan's distribution market is as efficient as those of other nations, how does one explain the spread in domestic and foreign prices? Second, Japanese consumers may not actually prefer a dense distribution of small retail stores because of their concern for service, since the existence of the restrictive Large-Scale Retail Store Law may suppress consumers' desire for large retail stores and low prices.

The Large-Scale Retail Store Law consequently came up for discussion at the SII talks. The law endeavors to protect smaller retailers by regulating the establishment of supermarkets and department stores with retail floor space of five hundred square meters or more and creates a forum (known as the Shochokyo) through which those seeking to build large retail stores must obtain the consent of neighborhood retailers before construction. Japan's regulations are stricter than those in France and West Germany, where similar laws regulate retail stores with floor space totaling one thousand square meters or more. The OECD Economic Survey argues that Japan's law is also applied to midsize retail stores.

The heightening of domestic and foreign criticism of the retail store law prompted the Japanese government to agree in the report of the SII talks to apply the current law more appropriately by limiting the period for considering the establishment of new stores to a minimum of one and a half years from the time business plans are announced.

Another problem that is frequently cited regarding Japan's distribution market is the establishment of distribution "affiliates" through exclusive agent contracts. The OECD Economic Survey states that the exclusive agent contract allows an importer or manufacturer to limit supply and thereby realize monopoly profits. The publication gives this system as one of the reasons for the high margins imposed on major consumer goods in Japan, such as for automobiles. The development of affiliate ties with distribution agents is frequently initiated by Japanese manufacturers. This makes it more difficult for foreign corporations to participate in Japan's markets unless they undertake the costly process of building their own exclusive agent networks.

One can hardly claim that adequate and conclusive research has taken place regarding Japan's distribution system. Rationalizing the system will take some time. In the meantime, it will be essential to implement policies, such as the reform of the Large-Scale Retail Store Law, that will create visible results. The basic goal should be a system that reflects market forces rather than government regulation.

The Competitiveness of Japan's Markets

Domestic industrial structures must adjust smoothly to changes in foreign exchange rates in order for a stronger yen and weaker dollar to quickly diminish Japanese and U.S. external imbalances. In other words, it is essential for labor and capital to promptly move from trade- to nontrade-goods industries in the nation whose currency has appreciated and for domestic demand to quickly shift from trade to nontrade goods. This will work rapidly to turn current account surplus down. The key to expeditious structural transformation is the degree to which resources, such as labor and capital, are mobile in the market and the degree of competitiveness in the market for production goods.

Kosai and others (1988) have compared the speed by which such factors as relative prices, employment, and investment adjust between the trade-goods and nontrade-goods sectors in response to foreign exchange rate fluctuations in Japan and the United States. While industrial adjustments occur relatively quickly in the United States, the process is not entirely smooth in Japan. Factors cited as causing this difference were the higher cost of labor mobility among industrial sectors (i.e., the income loss incurred when transferring jobs under a lifetime employment system), the existence of sectors where adjustment is difficult, and the lack of competition in domestic markets.

Are Japanese markets really less competitive than U.S. markets? Although it is no simple matter to establish a measure of market competitiveness, past research on Japanese and U.S. market concentration suggests that it is still too early to reach a definite conclusion.

Lawrence (1989) offers an interesting measure of incomplete markets. He argues that the greater the uncompetitiveness of a national market, the greater the likelihood that corporations will gain from making foreign direct investments. From this perspective, he concludes that the larger the proportion of intrafirm trade in its overall trade, the less competitive that national market is. He then notes that 49 percent of U.S. exports to Europe and 42 percent of U.S. imports from Europe consist of intrafirm trade. Corresponding figures for U.S. exports to and imports from Japan come to 72 and 75 percent, respectively. Of this, 58 and 66 percent, respectively, consist of intrafirm trade where the parent company is a Japanese firm. These are extremely high figures when compared to U.S. and European trade.

Furthermore, one must note that most direct investments concern downstream integration, wherein a manufacturing concern establishes marketing arms overseas. This tendency is confirmed in data regarding intrafirm trade between the United States and Europe. In addition to downstream integration, Japanese and U.S. intrafirm trade also occurs in a substantial number of cases of upstream integration, wherein a manufacturing firm sets up foreign companies from which to import raw materials and semifinished goods. This differs markedly from the normative pattern, underscoring the fact that it is cheaper to buy raw materials or to produce input materials outside of rather than in Japan.

Lawrence used such data to argue the incomplete nature of Japan's markets. On the other hand, of the total volume of U.S. exports to Japan, the share of exports that U.S. subsidiaries ship to their Japanese parent companies has declined dramatically since 1985. Lawrence considers this proof that Japanese markets are adjusting well to the stronger yen.

What sorts of policies should be established to increase competition with Japan's domestic markets? Kosai and others have proposed market-opening measures, the easing of regulations, and the promotion of domestic direct investments. They further emphasize the importance of ensuring that the benefits of an appreciating currency permeate the entire economy.

The easing of regulations, in particular, represents a cornerstone of the domestic policies of the Reagan and Thatcher administrations, a policy area where Japan's slow-footedness is conspicuous. The OECD's *Economic Survey: Japan 1987/88* states in effect that regulatory reach in Japan is broad and that heavily regulated industries account for about a quarter of the nation's economy. Furthermore, while commending the recent trend toward privatization in Japan, the publication specifies that efforts to dismantle regulations have not been as energetic as those in the United States and Great Britain. The OECD survey examines such sectors as real estate and housing, distribution, transportation (airlines, the former Japan National Railway, and trucking), and telecommunications as sectors where public regulation and intervention have restrained competition. It concludes that it would be appropriate to overhaul a number of regulations that restrict or weaken market forces in the transportation and distribution sectors. And since the benefits of having more market-driven industries would be enormous, it contends that the process of deregulation must not be hindered by vested interests.

Although it is unclear to what extent external imbalances will narrow once the easing of regulations amplifies market competitiveness, there is no doubt that relevant measures will be most effective in securing the structural adjustment of the Japanese and U.S. economies over the long haul.

4. The Need for a New Maekawa Report

The Maekawa Report, released in 1986 by a private advisory group of the former Prime Minister Yasuhiro Nakasone, is serving as an important blueprint for developing policies that will promote structural adjustments in Japan.[5] Furthermore, discussions between the Japanese and U.S. governments regarding individual policy issues—or the so-called Structural Impediments Initiative (SII)—culminated in the release of a binational report in July 1990. Through this process, the two countries have agreed on concrete policy measures that Japan will adopt and on a time frame for their implementation.

The Maekawa Report seeks to change the current social and economic framework through such steps as easing various regulations and reducing working hours. Such changes are then to become the basis for ameliorating external imbalances through domestic demand expansion and for improving the economic well-being of Japanese citizens. As such, the report aptly describes the direction Japan must travel in achieving structural adjustments.

The Maekawa Report is also noteworthy in that, however vague, it is the only blueprint for structural adjustments that has emerged from the leading industrial nations. Some, however, have criticized the SII process as revealing the Japanese government's continuing need for foreign pressure before effecting changes. Others have reacted strongly against the United States in their belief that the SII process represents interference in

Japan's domestic affairs. However, a *Nihon Keizai Shimbun* survey, carried out in the midst of the SII talks, indicates that a majority of Japanese citizens felt that the United States was making reasonable demands regarding the revision of the Large-Scale Retail Store Law and the reform of the land tax system. The SII agreement can be commended as a continuation of the direction first outlined by the Maekawa Report.

Nevertheless, certain improvements are needed with respect to the way in which structural adjustments are currently progressing. First, Japanese domestic prices must be reduced to international levels to eliminate the divergence between domestic and foreign prices. This is imperative in order to ensure that structural adjustments will bear meaningful results both domestically and internationally.

As described above, the reasons for the divergence in domestic and foreign prices are both complex and controversial. Even so, as this price gap points to the existence of structural distortions, efforts to narrow it constitute a significant policy issue. Japan must establish the correction of these and foreign price differentials as a medium-term policy goal and must develop comprehensive measures toward realizing this goal.

Specific medium-term targets were not a part of the Maekawa Report. Despite the fact that, by their very nature, such policies require a considerable period of time to implement, the SII talks focused for the most part on short-term policy issues. This indicates the need to clearly articulate the elimination of the spread between domestic and foreign prices as a medium-term policy goal and to publicize a new structural adjustments program consisting of a suitable long-term policy schedule. In short, Japan should independently formulate a new Maekawa Report.

Despite the widespread support among Japanese citizens for the original Maekawa Report, efforts to implement its guidelines provoked strong resistance from the bureaucracy and groups with vested interests because the report lacked specific policy measures. As a result, the development of effective policies did not occur. One cannot deny that U.S. prodding, in the form of the Structural Impediments Initiative, was needed to prompt final implementation of the Maekawa Report. To avoid such a situation in the future, it is imperative that the new Maekawa Report be developed with a clear medium-term policy goal, specific policy recommendations, and a corresponding time schedule.

To promote economic structural adjustments in the 1990s, it is necessary to consider the decline in Japan's potential capacity for economic growth. Previous research suggests that two supply shocks—labor shortages and higher energy prices—will reduce Japan's potential economic growth rate to 2.9 to 3.4 percent during the first half of the 1990s, compared to 4.3 percent for the 1980s. Such a projected decrease will affect the structural adjustment process in both positive and negative ways. Generally speaking, a slowdown in economic growth increases the difficulty of persuading groups that might be adversely affected by policy adjustments, prolonging Japan's response to foreign pressure. Slower growth, on the other hand, will enhance the need for the efficient distribution of resources (such as the vitalization of nonefficient, protected sectors), thereby increasing domestic pressure for the easing of regulations. This indicates that the structural adjustment process should begin to depend more on domestic pressure than on foreign pressure in the coming years.

Japan is expected to face serious labor shortages throughout the 1990s. The issue of accepting foreign workers is consequently beginning to surface as a new topic for the structural adjustment process. Japan's working-age population formerly expanded at an annual pace of about nine hundred thousand. Demographic changes, however, have reduced this by about half in recent years. The working-age population is actually forecast to stop growing in the mid-1990s and to shrink in the latter half of the decade.[6]

Many experts believe the addition of more women and older workers to the labor force will help overcome labor shortages. The Japanese government adopts a similar point of view in rejecting unskilled foreign labor. Even so, more than one hundred thousand foreign workers (including undocumented laborers) are estimated to be already working in Japan, and the demand is projected to climb. Japan has had a homogeneous labor force, but the future will require a new form of economic structural adjustment encompassing a broad range of issues, such as management practices and the maintenance of social order.[7]

5. Beyond Patterned Pluralism

Highly developed economies are associated with intricate and complex power politics. Attempts to change the social framework, such as efforts to ease regulations or to make systemic changes, cannot avoid arousing powerful forces in opposition. Although consumers are large in number, they generally find it difficult to unite around specific economic objectives. For many changes, the beneficiaries are diffuse, but the losers are clearly recognizable, and they unite in opposing change and seek common political goals. As a consequence, they have frequently found their interests sacrificed for those of particular protected industries.

This is true of all nations. Some domestic and foreign analysts have wondered, therefore, why Japan appears to lag behind other industrial nations in promoting social changes that will increase the well-being of consumers, such as easing import regulations and reviewing the protection of domestic industries. This appearance, however, is often based on misunderstandings. As Japanese government policymakers have stressed over many years, Japan's imports markets are not as closed as is generally believed. Regulations remain on the import of twenty-one agricultural products. Although this surpasses the number of similar regulations in the United States, it cannot be said to be excessive when compared to Europe.

Nevertheless, clearly, the overthrow of vested interests that have once established themselves is particularly difficult in Japan. Real estate prices, the distribution market, and Japanese business practices, topics that were raised at the SII talks, have all been the target of domestic debate for many years. Even so, such debate has seldom resulted in the implementation of effective policy measures. Researchers of Japanese politics have frequently referred to the social system that stands behind Japan's economic structure as "patterned pluralism."

Japan is unquestionably a democratic nation. Although some industries and corporations retain immense political power (e.g., agriculture and some major corporate groups), other industries as well as consumers are extremely weak. Therefore, even though it exists, pluralism is rather restricted in Japan. This has led to Japan being called a nation of patterned pluralism. Currently, the political decision-making process in Japan is dominated by three groups: business sectors with political muscle, their representatives in the Diet (so-called *zoku* legislators), and the bureaucrats who oversee industry. These groups seek to maintain a symmetry of power and to protect their vested interests, an interrelationship that has been called an iron triangle. Reflecting this, the budgetary process has for a considerable period of time consisted of making incremental increases to past budget allocations in deference to vested interests.

Similarly, in the economic sphere some researchers emphasize that although Japan is a capitalistic nation, patterned pluralism distinguishes Japan from other industrialized economies. There is no doubt that a sound market mechanism exists for transactions involving most goods and services, and competition is extremely intense. Consumers are exceedingly demanding regarding product quality and price, and Japanese corporations compete vigorously to supply markets with superior products. At the macroeconomic level, consumption and investment patterns in Japan respond far more sensitively than in Europe and the United States to changes in such economic variables as interest rates and tax rates. However, for agriculture and other regulated industrial sectors (e.g., some areas of transportation and telecommunications), the market mechanism does not function fully. In this sense, pluralism (meaning unhampered markets) is functionally patterned in certain limited areas of Japan's economy.

In order to improve their economic well-being, Japanese consumers must remedy their nation's patterned pluralism and promote appropriate loosening of regulations and systemic reform. Nevertheless, the existence of patterned pluralism has made it difficult to defeat vested interests in the political arena. In this context external pressure, such as the SII talks, has helped to buttress the shortcomings of patterned pluralism. U.S. demands that were asserted in the SII context found wide support among Japanese citizens due to their recognition that external pressure offers an effective means for surmounting patterned pluralism. Even so, it is inconceivable that external pressure alone would be sufficient to push domestic systems and policies in a desirable direction. Japan must have a built-in mechanism that allows social change to take place autonomously. In other words, economic structural adjustments must be complemented by changes to Japan's social system.

Regarding those issues directly associated with economic policy, three trigger mechanisms can be suggested that will assist in the reform of patterned pluralism.

First, consumer groups that truly represent consumer interests must be fostered. Some major consumer groups currently exist in Japan. As of yet, however, none of them support the full-fledged liberalization of the import of rice and other agricultural products. Only one of these major consumer groups came out clearly in favor of the 1989 consumption tax, which many economists viewed as serving the interests of consumers. Such groups must be able to effectively lobby the Japanese government regarding the opening of domestic markets and must be able to make resolute demands on foreign corporations that prefer to criticize Japan while ignoring their own lack of effort.

Second, there is a need to reform the political system so that the will of the Japanese people is directly reflected in the political decision-making process. Led by the Liberal Democratic Party, discussions are currently underway concerning the reform of Japan's electoral system. Reform will basically center around the establishment of single representative electoral districts, which is envisioned as leading to a system wherein two major political parties, both capable of holding the reins of government, compete in presenting their policies to voters, as is the case in the United States and Great Britain. Even so, there is no guarantee that such an electoral change will bring about a meaningful policy formulation process. More important is to make broadly available to Japanese citizens information related to policy formulation, which is currently the monopoly of the civil service. This should also be accompanied by a change from the current system to one in which actual policy is determined responsibly by the representatives of Japanese citizens in the Diet, Japan's legislature. As a practical first step, senior-level civil service positions (e.g., director general of the bureau of each ministry and above) should be filled by political appointees. Furthermore, the defense of government policy in the Diet should be restricted to elected officials. Japan's civil service system has usually been effective in achieving the policy goals assigned to it. Nevertheless, changes are called for from the medium- and long-term perspective in order to bring about the realization of a more broadly pluralistic democratic system.

Third, the smooth management of a more broadly pluralistic society will require the development of a sound "third sector" that is capable of providing policy analysis from a neutral standpoint. It is natural for groups in support of and in opposition to particular policy issues to clash vigorously with each other in any pluralistic society. Such a situation demands the existence of a neutral third sector, independent of government and industry, to present policy analysis from the perspective of the national economy and to clarify policy choices. Many political and economic research centers have been established in Japan in recent years, for the most part by financial institutions. Research centers that can be said to carry out policy analysis from a neutral standpoint, however, have yet to appear.

Notes

1. How structural adjustments or structural changes are understood will differ entirely according to which sorts of economic variables and consequent configurations of structural parameters are thought to represent the entire economy, or according to the sort of economic model premised. As a result, it is extremely difficult to give a proper definition of "structural adjustments" and "structural changes." Furthermore, discussions of structural adjustments are prone to take place without a necessary focus. Even if a particular economic model is premised and structural adjustments—meaning changes to structural parameters—are debated, considerable doubt has been cast, particularly by macroeconomic policy experts, as to whether government policies can actually affect structural parameters.

2. The Maekawa Report also contains nonstructural adjustment policies if we adopt the strict definition of "structural adjustments" as "making changes to structural parameters."

3. *Tekenaka-Ogawa* (A Macroeconomic Analysis of External Imbalances) (Tokyo: Toyo-Keizai, 1987).

4. Yukio Noguchi, "Land Problem of Japan" (in Japanese), in M. Ito, K. Ueda, and H. Takenaka, eds., *Perspectives on the Japanese Economy* (Tokyo: Chikumashobo, 1988), 225–42.

5. Prime Minister Yasuhiro Nakasone carried out the privatization of Japan National Railway and Nippon Telegraph and Telephone during the latter half of the 1980s. Although these measures were not included in the recommendations of the Maekawa Report, the privatization of these two government-held companies can be considered a part of economic structural adjustment and international harmonization.

6. "Labor-shortage bankruptcy" is a new phase gaining currency in Japan. It refers to a situation wherein sufficient demand exists but an inadequate labor supply forces a company to close its doors. Labor-shortage bankruptcies are on the rise among companies unable to move abroad to secure workers. They include firms in the construction industry, consumer services, and some of the smallest firms in the manufacturing sector.

7. Sufficient analysis and debate have not taken place, even among labor economists, regarding the outlook for labor supply and demand in Japan. The government and those favoring Japanese-style management practices strongly oppose the acceptance of foreign labor, particularly unskilled labor. One likely reason for this opposition is the concern that an increase of foreign workers will create social instability because of Japan's undeveloped urban policies. However, Japan is facing a serious labor shortage, most notably for unskilled labor, and this has led to some in the business community, primarily among small and midsize businesses, to appeal strongly for foreign labor. Even if women and older people are actively brought into the labor market, this alone will be insufficient to overcome labor shortages. The time is ap-

proaching when the full-fledged acceptance of foreign workers will become necessary.

References

Kosai, Y., et al. 1988. *2000 nen eno Sekai Keizai Tenbo* (World Economic Prospect for 2000). Tokyo: Economic Planning Agency.
Lawrence, R. 1989. "How Open Is Japan?" Prepared for the NBER-Sponsored Conference on the U.S. and Japan: Trade and Investment.

Contributors

Yoichi Funabashi is the Washington Bureau chief of the *Asahi Shimbun,* a leading Japanese daily. He has covered politics and economics in Japan for twenty years and has been the *Asahi* correspondent in Washington, D.C., and Beijing, and a Nieman fellow at Harvard University. Funabashi was an Ushiba fellow in 1986 and was a fellow at the Institute for International Economics in 1987. He is the author of several books, including *The Theory of Economic Security* (1978), *Neibu: Inside China* (1983), and *The U.S.–Japan Economic Entanglement: The Inside Story* (1987). Winner of the Suntory Humanities Award of 1983, he was also awarded the 1985 Vaughn-Ueda Prize—often called Japan's Pulitzer Prize—for his coverage of U.S.–Japan economic friction, and the Yoshino Sakuzo Award in 1988 for his book *Managing the Dollar: From the Plaza to the Louvre.*

Takatoshi Ito is currently a professor at the Institute of Economic Research, Hitotsubashi University, having been associate professor there from 1988 to 1991. Educated at Hitotsubashi University, he continued his studies at Harvard University with a scholarship from the Japan Society for the Promotion of Science and received his Ph.D. in Economics in 1979. Ito then accepted a position as associate professor of economics at the University of Minnesota and later became a research fellow at Stanford University, a visiting associate professor at Harvard University's Economics Department, and a visiting research fellow at the

187

International Monetary Fund. He is presently affiliated with the National Bureau of Economic Research, the American Economic Association, and the Econometric Society. Ito has written extensively in English and Japanese, and his publications include *Economic Analysis of Disequilibrium: Theory and Empirical Analysis* (in Japanese), which was awarded at the twenty-ninth Nikkei Economics Book Award in November 1986.

Heizo Takenaka is currently an associate professor at Keio University. He was born in 1951 and began his career at the Japan Development Bank after graduating from Hitotsubashi University. He was a visiting scholar at Harvard University and the University of Pennsylvania during the period 1981–82 and then served as a senior economist at the Ministry of Finance's Institute of Fiscal and Monetary Policy before joining the faculty of Osaka University. In 1988–89, he was awarded the Ushiba Fellowship to study at Washington's Institute for International Economics before assuming his current position. His publications include *The Role of Investment for Energy Conservation: Future Japanese Growth and Energy Economics* (1981) and *Japan–U.S. Economic Controversy* (1988), in which he comprehensively surveys economic friction between Japan and the United States.

Akihiko Tanaka is associate professor of international relations at the University of Tokyo, a position he has held since 1984. Upon graduating from the University of Tokyo's faculty of liberal arts in 1977, Tanaka transferred to the Massachusetts Institute of Technology and received his Ph.D. in political science in 1981. Upon returning to Japan, he became a researcher at the Research Institute for Peace and Security. During 1983, he worked as a research assistant at the University of Tokyo before assuming his current position in 1984. Tanaka was an exchange scholar at the Ruhr Universität Bochum in 1986.

Taizo Yakushiji is professor of political science and international relations at Keio University. Until 1991, he was professor of technology and international relations at the Graduate Institute of Policy Science at Saitama University. He was educated at Keio University, the University of Tokyo, and the Massachusetts Institute of Technology, where he received his Ph.D. in political science. Yakushiji studied in the United

States as a Fulbright scholar and Ford Foundation fellow from 1970 to 1975. His publications include *Reshuffling Firms for Technology?*, *The American and Japanese Auto Industries in Transition*, *Tekuno-hegemoni*, and *Kokyo-Seisaku*. Yakushiji is also coauthor, with James MacNeill and Pieter Winsemius, of the Trilateral Commission's 1980 task force report, *Beyond Interdependence: The Meshing of the World's Economy and the Earth's Ecology*.

Kazumasa Iwata is a professor at the University of Tokyo. Upon graduating from the department of international relations at the University of Tokyo in 1970, he joined the Economic Planning Agency. From 1972 to 1973 he studied at the Institute for World Economy in Kiel, attending the Post-Dokteranden Seminar. He became administrator of the Monetary and Fiscal Policy Division in the Department of Economics and Statistics at the OECD in 1976 and served at that post for three years. Iwata has been a visiting fellow at the Australian University, an honored visiting professor at the University of Alberta, and a visiting professor at the Economic Growth Center of Yale University. Before becoming an associate professor at the University of Tokyo, he was senior economist at the Economic Research Institute of the Economic Planning Agency. His book *Monetary Policy and Banking Behavior* received the Economist Prize in 1981, and his recent publications include *International Economics* (1990) and "Capital Cost of Business Investment in Japan and the United States under Tax Reform," in *Japan and the World Economy*, no. 2 (1990).

Makoto Sakurai has been the director-general and senior economist at the Mitsui Marine Research Institute since 1989. He graduated from Chuo University's department of economics in 1969 and received a Ph.D. in economics from the University of Tokyo in 1976. Later that year, he joined the Export-Import Bank of Japan. From 1980 to 1982, he was visiting fellow at the Economic Growth Center at Yale University. In 1982, he was appointed senior economist of the Research Institute of Overseas Investment at the Export-Import Bank of Japan. Among his recent publications are "Nihon no Kaigai Chokusetsu Toshi no Doko to Kettei Yoin" (Trends in Japan's Overseas Direct Investment and Its Determinants) in *Kaigai Toshi Kenyusho-Ho* (Monthly Report of the Research Institute, Export-Import Bank of Japan) and "20-nen wo Mukaeru ASEAN to Kongo no Tainichi Kankei" (ASEAN after Twenty Years and Its Relations with Japan) in *Kaigai Toshi Kenkyusho-Ho*. Sakurai was also one of the working paper authors for "The United States and Japan: Cooperative Leadership for Peace and Global Prosperity—A Report by a Committee of Six," jointly sponsored by the Atlantic Council of the United States, the Bretton Woods Committee, and JCIE.

Index